Oxford
A Very Peculiar History™

With added Honours

'I wonder anyone does anything at Oxford but
dream and remember, the place is so beautiful.
One almost expects the people to sing instead
of speaking. It is all ... like an opera.'

W. B. Yeats

For Chris Wright,
who knows what's Hwaet!

DA

Editor: Stephen Haynes

Cover artist: David Antram
Additional artwork: Shutterstock

Published in Great Britain in MMXIV by
Book House, an imprint of
The Salariya Book Company Ltd
25 Marlborough Place, Brighton BN1 1UB
www.salariya.com

ISBN: 978-1-908973-81-8

SCRIBO   BOOK HOUSE   SCRIBBLERS

3 5 7 9 8 6 4 2

A CIP catalogue record for this book is available
from the British Library.

Printed and bound in China.
Printed on paper from sustainable sources
Reprinted in MMXVIII.

Visit
www.salariya.com
for our online catalogue and
free fun stuff.

Oxford

A Very Peculiar History™

With added Honours

Written by
David Arscott

Created and designed by
David Salariya

BOOK HOUSE
a SALARIYA imprint

'Oxford lends sweetness to labour
and dignity to leisure.'
Henry James

'Oxford is the most dangerous place
to which a young man can be sent.'
Anthony Trollope

'I was a modest, good-humoured boy. It is
Oxford that has made me insufferable.'
Max Beerbohm

'A sanctuary in which exploded systems
and obsolete prejudices find shelter and
protection after they have been hunted
out of every corner of the world.'
Adam Smith

'You will hear more good things on the
outside of a stagecoach from London to
Oxford than if you were to pass a twelve-
month with the undergraduates, or heads
of colleges, of that famous university.'
William Hazlitt

Contents

Ten things to thank Oxford for

1. **The first Bible in English**, courtesy of John Wycliffe (1320–1384), a scholar at Balliol and later its master. The Catholic Church was far from thankful, however, regarding him as a heretic: 44 years after his death, the Pope had his bones dug up and cremated.

2. *Alice in Wonderland* and *Alice Through the Looking-Glass*, by Charles Lutwidge Dodgson (1832–1898), a.k.a. Lewis Carroll, a scholar and later mathematics lecturer at Christ Church.

3. **Oxford marmalade** No breakfast table should be without this world-famous preserve, which can be seen down the rabbit hole in the first illustrations for *Alice*. It was an essential for Scott on his Antarctic expedition: a jar was later found buried in the polar ice.

4. **The Morris Minor** Forget Volkswagen – this was the British 'people's car', made at Cowley by William Morris, later Lord Nuffield (1877–1963). The first Minor appeared in 1928; the more familiar 'beetle'-shaped model, a.k.a. the Morris 1000, was made from 1948 to 1972.

5. **The Oxford Movement** University men were prominent in the Victorian High Church 'smells and bells' practices which developed into Anglo-Catholicism. John Wycliffe would have turned in his grave – if he'd still had one.

6. **The Boat Race** The exhausting struggle with Cambridge began in 1829, has been held on the Thames in London annually since 1856 (wartime apart), and still holds the public imagination today.

7. **Oxfam** Founded in 1942 as the Oxford Committee for Famine Relief, the humanitarian organisation today works in some 90 countries worldwide.

8. **Oxford bags** These commodious trousers had their heyday from the 1920s to the 1950s, but enjoyed a revival in the 1970s when the Bay City Rollers sported a cut-off tartan version.

9. **The 4-minute mile** They run 1,500 metres these days, but Roger Bannister's time of 3 minutes 59.4 seconds at the Iffley Road Track on 6 May 1954 was an athletic feat some experts had once thought impossible.

10. **Spoonerisms** The comical switching of initial consonants between two words ('Three cheers for our queer old dean!') was the accidental habit of a New College warden, the Reverend William Spooner (1844–1930). Most of the examples usually atttributed to him are apocryphal, among them his supposed dismissal of a wayward student: 'You have hissed all my mystery lectures and tasted a whole worm. Kindly leave Oxford on the next town drain.'

Putting Oxford on the map

1. c. 1000 Church of St Michael at the North Gate built as part of Saxon defences.
2. 1071 Oxford Castle begun; the motte (mound) and St George's Tower survive.
3. 1130 Beaumont Palace built by Henry I: birthplace of kings Richard I (1157) and John (1166). The palace is no longer extant but gives its name to Beaumont Street.
4. 1288 Merton College's Mob Quad built; claimed to be the oldest in the university.
5. 1427–1483 Divinity School, now part of the Bodleian Library, is the university's first major building project. It is famous for its spectacular vaulted ceiling.
6. 1545 Henry VIII makes Christ Church chapel the cathedral of a new diocese.
7. 1555–1556 Protestant martyrs Latimer, Cranmer and Ridley burned at the stake in the Broad. The Martyrs' Memorial (7a) is built in nearby St Giles' in 1843.
8. 1790 Oxford Canal completed; wharves extended to where Nuffield College is now.
9. 1844 The railway comes to Oxford; the station moves to its present site in 1852.
10. 1860 Great evolution debate at the new Museum of Natural History.
11. 1878 Lady Margaret Hall, the first women's college, is established.
12. 1913 William Morris (later Lord Nuffield) establishes his motor works at Cowley.
13. 1954 Roger Bannister breaks the 4-minute mile at Iffley Road running track.
14. 2009 Ashmolean Museum (first opened on its present site in 1845) reopens after a major refurbishment. In 2013 it acquires Millais's portrait of John Ruskin.

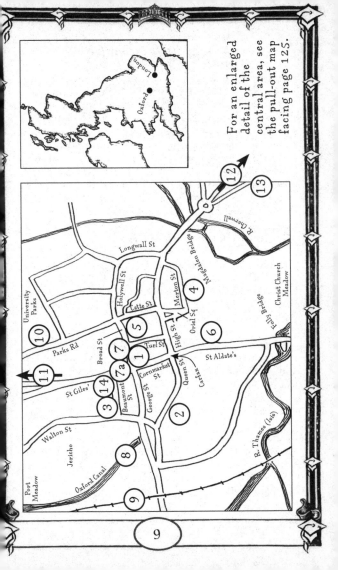

For an enlarged detail of the central area, see the pull-out map facing page 125.

A miracle worker

St Frideswide, the patron saint of both the city and the university, is said to have founded a priory in the early 8th century on the site of today's Christ Church Cathedral. Legend has it that she was a Mercian princess who took a vow of chastity, and that she was pursued by a lustful prince who was providentially struck blind when he attempted to take her by force. Frideswide prayed for the restoration of his sight, after which he wisely agreed to leave her alone. Many more miracles followed.

After the priory was destroyed during the St Brice's Day massacre of 1002 (see page 23), a monastery of Augustinian canons rose among the ruins, and in 1180 – with King Henry II in attendance – the archbishop of Canterbury installed the saint's remains within a shrine in the monastery church.

She was not, alas, allowed to rest in peace. In 1546, following the Dissolution of the Monasteries, the church became Oxford's cathedral. James Calfhill, a Calvinist canon during Elizabeth I's reign, had her bones mingled with those of Catherine Dammartin, a former nun whose marriage to the Protestant theologian Peter Martyr Vermigli had scandalised the Roman Catholic church. Catherine's bones had been disinterred and flung on a dungheap, and theories differ as to whether Calfhill was saving them for posterity or desecrating the shrine in order to prevent a cult of St Frideswide developing.

INTRODUCTION

What makes Oxford special?

An intellectual transit camp for young scholars, the focus of wistful memories for countless thousands of their predecessors around the globe, Oxford is as much a place of imagination and desire as it is an undeniably modern city of 150,000 souls, many of them going about their workaday business just as if they lived in Oldham, Oswestry or Oundle.

The very stones seem to breathe romance. Come in from the suburbs and Matthew Arnold's 'dreaming spires' present a scarcely believable medieval townscape at the centre.

> 'The truth is that Oxford is simply a very beautiful city in which it is convenient to segregate a certain number of the young of the nation while they are growing up.'
>
> *Evelyn Waugh*

While the non-academic history of Oxford will be given its due in these pages (from Dane-bothered Saxons to today's motorworks in Cowley), we don't apologise for skewing the emphasis towards cap and gown. Who, after all, would begrudge the appearance of such a colourful cast of characters, even if some have merely flitted through in order to earn their degrees? Their restless brilliance is essential to the Oxford story.

A few facts and figures:

- **There are over 23,000 students at the University of Oxford and a further 18,000 at Oxford Brookes University, which began as an art school in 1865, later became a polytechnic and was given university status in 1992. Of the total, roughly 34,000 are full-time undergraduates or postgraduates.**

- In the 2001 census, 26 per cent of the working-age population were students – the highest proportion anywhere in England and Wales. Apart from the centre, most live to the north around the Woodstock and Banbury Roads and to the east around Cowley Road and Headington.

- The population turnover of Oxford is 25 per cent each year – the highest for any English local authority area.

- There's an extra influx of 26,000 people who come into the city every day to work, and 9.5 million tourists arrive every year to gawp.

Two rivers

Oxford has two rivers – although you might easily be fooled into thinking that it had three.

To the east of the town, the Cherwell (pronounced 'Charwell') flows south through the University Parks, under Magdalen Bridge and through Christ Church Meadow before joining the mightier Thames.

The Thames is known locally as the Isis – hence the possible confusion. There was a ford for oxen in Saxon times (perhaps in the vicinity of today's Folly Bridge), and this gave the town its name.

Oxford and Cambridge

The two ancient universities together known as 'Oxbridge' are the Tweedledum and Tweedledee of the education world. Though dark-blue Oxford (short form: Oxon) has traditionally veered towards the humanities and light-blue Cambridge (Cantab) to the sciences, the differences are far less marked than what they have in common:

- **A collegiate system.** The exams are set by the university, which also presents the lectures, but students enrol at one of the many colleges, which is where they have their...

- **Tutorials** (known as 'supervisions' at Cambridge). Weekly sessions with a tutor, often on a one-to-one basis, are a valued feature of Oxbridge scholarship.

- **Venerable medieval buildings** surrounding grassy quads – or 'courts' in the other place.

- **Their own publishing houses:** Oxford University Press (OUP) and Cambridge University Press (CUP).

- **Debating societies.** Aspiring politicians make a beeline for the Oxford and Cambridge Unions.

- **World-class museums:** the Ashmolean at Oxford and the Fitzwilliam at Cambridge.

- **Botanic gardens.** Oxford's was founded in 1621, Cambridge's 210 years later.

- **Theatrical societies:** the Oxford University Dramatic Society (OUDS) and the Oxford Revue; the Cambridge University Amateur Dramatic Club, the Marlowe Society and Cambridge Footlights.

- **Business schools:** the Saïd at Oxford and the Judge at Cambridge.

- **Legal-deposit libraries.** The Bodleian at Oxford and Cambridge University Library are each entitled to a free copy of every book and periodical published in the UK.

- **Science parks.** Oxford's was founded by Magdalen College and Prudential plc in 1990.

- **Academic dress.** This includes gowns and mortarboards (or caps for women) and is *de rigueur* on formal occasions – but Cambridge no longer dresses up for examinations.

- **Punting on the rivers** – though the techniques are different: the Oxford style is to regard the open end as the stern of the vessel and to stand in it while pushing down on the pole, whereas Cambridge punters stand on the decking (or 'till'), with the open end forward.

The locals, as we shall see, haven't always been enamoured of the bright young bloods in their midst – sometimes with good reason – although any lingering friction today is as nothing compared with the rioting in medieval times, which resulted in murders and hangings. (Cambridge, marginally the younger of the two venerable seats of learning, is said to have been founded by Oxford students on the run from vengeful townsmen.)

Holy grail

Since Oxford is for so many a place of dreams, it's fitting that the beguiling legend of King Arthur and his Round Table should have taken its potent and enduring medieval form here.

The stories of questing chivalric knights and a once and future king who would return to save his country were embroidered by Geoffrey of Monmouth, an Oxford don, in his *Historia Regum Britanniae* (*History of the Kings of Britain*), written in the 1130s.

More than 200 manuscripts of the *Historia* survive, and it still inspires writers, artists and film-makers almost 900 years after Geoffrey put pen to parchment.

Today's more relaxed mingling of town and gown perhaps owes something to the growth in the number of women undergraduates from around one in six during the 1960s to the current 50 per cent – a profound change which gives the lie to any suggestion that the university is a sadly mouldering institution set in academic aspic.

But of course not! Those honey-coloured quads are home to some of the keenest minds in the arts and sciences, a community of learned fellows and tutors constantly challenged, amused and perplexed by the demands of their charges, that ever-shifting throng of turbulent and testing teenagers.

Between them they bring vitality to an Oxford which, while it may be ancient, is forever new.

Oxford's oldest building

The North Gate, incorporating the Bocardo
gaol, stood at the north end of Cornmarket
Street until 1771. To the right is the tower
of St Michael at the North Gate (c.1000),
the oldest surviving building in the city.
The shops in the right foreground
are still thriving.

ALFRED THE GREAT AND ALL THAT

Early Oxford was a frontier town, a strongly walled Saxon refuge against marauding Vikings from the Danelaw – the territory, with its capital at York, which was occupied by the Danes and encompassed East Anglia, the eastern part of the old kingdom of Mercia and large swathes of northern England.

After King Alfred of Wessex won a great victory over the invaders in May 878, he built a string of 33 fortresses (or *burhs*) to ensure that the Danes should go no further – and Oxford was a vital link in the chain.

What had people been doing here before? The evidence is decidedly patchy:

- Archaeologists excavating the site of the former Radcliffe Infirmary (just north of the city centre) in 2009 discovered evidence of prehistoric settlement on a gravel terrace deposited on the floodplain of the upper Thames valley.

- Bronze and Iron Age people successively occupied Port Meadow, which has been described as 'Oxford's oldest monument', complete with an array of banks and ditches.

- The Romans seem to have used a river crossing at North Hinksey, to the west, and they had significant pottery works at Cowley, but they didn't see fit to strike one of their impressive metalled roads through what is now Oxford.

- St Frideswide (see page 10) founded a priory on the east bank of the Thames early in the 8th century, and a clay bank or artificial causeway spanned the Thames just north of today's Folly Bridge, but any lay settlement close to the monastic pile was very slow to develop.

Alfred's new burh, on the other hand, soon grew to become a thriving centre, its river crossing allowing a growing north–south trade between the Midlands and the port of Southampton – although the town's first historical mention (in the *Anglo-Saxon Chronicle* entry for 911) emphasises its early vulnerability. Until that year it had been a part of beleaguered Mercia, held by the Saxons but in the front line of the vicious cut-and-thrust. Now it came under the control of Alfred's son and successor, Edward the Elder, who would soon advance deep into Danish territory.

During the reign of Edward's son Athelstan, who unified the country under Wessex rule (a royal chronicler boasted that there was 'peace and abundance of all things') Oxford had a mint and four moneyers.

At the crossroads

The original layout of the fortified settlement is largely lost to us because of later growth, including the building of new defences in Norman times, but we know where to begin: Carfax (from the French *carrefour*, 'crossroads') was, and remains, the heart of the place. The four present roads ran from here to gates in the surrounding walls.

The burh was small and perhaps designed as a square. A likely scenario is that the northern rampart ran along the line of Ship Street, as it was still to do in medieval times; the southern section just north of St Frideswide's (now Christ Church); the western along the line of New Inn Hall Street and St Ebbe's Street; and the eastern just west of Catte Street and Magpie Lane. There were four main gates and four smaller ones.

Each of the main gates had its own church: St Michael at the north gate, St Aldate's at the south, St Peter-le-Bailey at the west and St Mary the Virgin at the east.

Carfax Tower

That marooned tower at the northwest corner of Carfax has had a proud history as part of the city church of Oxford, St Martin's. From around 1122 until 1896 this was the place where the mayor and other local worthies processed to worship, but it eventually became a bit of a nuisance among an increasingly busy throng of traffic. All but the tower was pulled down, and the honour of being the 'city church' passed to All Saints in the High Street.

There seems to have been a royal residence in Oxford at this period, because Edward the Elder's son Alfweard died here in August 924 – just weeks after his father, and before he could be crowned king in his place.

Massacre

Now we fast forward to St Brice's Day (13 November) 1002, when that ill-advised, or witless, monarch Ethelred the Unready reacted to a spate of renewed Viking raids by ordering the death of all Danish people in Saxon England. These foreigners were, he later claimed in defence of his brutality, 'sprouting like cockle [a weed] among the wheat'.

Oxford wasn't the only town to heed the call, but nowhere else seems to have witnessed so much bloodletting. Many of the terrified Danes retreated inside St Frideswide's Church, but the zealous locals simply burned it down with their helpless victims inside.

Ethelred issued a royal charter in 1004, in which he explained, in weasel words, why he had needed to rebuild the church. The Danes, he said, had broken the doors and bolts to enter 'this sanctuary of Christ', but their pursuers fired the place after having being 'forced by necessity' to assault them.

Among the victims of Ethelred's grim anti-Dane day was Gunhilde, a sister of the Viking leader Sweyn Forkbeard. She was put to death despite special pleading that she should be spared, and her brother's revenge was to be far from sweet.

Danish dead

In 2008 an excavation at St John's College unearthed the skeletons of 37 male Danes between the ages of 16 and 25, all with signs of terrible injuries and carbon-dated to between 960 and 1020.

The first thought was that they were victims of the St Brice's Day Massacre, but later research revealed that they were taller and more robust than average Danes of the time, that their bones showed signs of healed scars as well as fatal injuries, and that they had eaten vast amounts of seafood – suggesting that they may have been a Viking warrior band, defeated in battle before being rounded up and mercilessly put to death.

- Sweyn made repeated attacks on England and had to be bought off with huge amounts of the bribery known as *Danegeld* ('Dane-money').

- In 1009 the Vikings sacked Oxford, burning much of it to the ground. In the rebuilding, the town walls were extended east and west to incorporate suburban sprawl.

- In 1013 Ethelred fled to Normandy and, after Sweyn's death the following year, was allowed to return only after promising to practise 'good government'.

- Any relief was shortlived. Soon after Ethelred died in 1016, Sweyn's son Canute (or Cnut) became king. He was crowned that Christmas in London, with the nobility confirming their allegiance the following month – in Oxford.

Oxford at this time was the seat of a kind of national debating chamber, located geographically between the two powers of Wessex and Saxon Mercia without being committed to either of them. A 'great council' in 1015 brought together nobles from all parts of the country, including, remarkably, thegns (members of the lesser nobility) from the Danish boroughs in eastern Mercia – that is, part of the Danelaw.

Two of these thegns were treacherously killed during the session, which understandably brought about a rift between Wessex and the Danelaw, yet by 1018 another council was able to establish a treaty of friendship between Canute's followers and those of the English who had originally opposed him.

On the king's death in 1035 it was at Oxford that a council met to consider the succession. The throne was claimed by two of Canute's sons, the half-brothers Harold Harefoot (the choice of the Midland thegns and the shipmen of London) and Harthacanute (championed by Wessex). The two shared the crown for a time before Harefoot eventually won out.

Royal Headington

King Ethelred had a palace at Headington, though how grand it was, it's impossible to know. His charter of 1004, which not only defended the St Brice's Day Massacre, but gave a quarry and surrounding land in Headington to St Frideswide's Priory, was recorded as 'written in the royal vill [manor] which is called Headington'.

Another Oxford council was called in 1065, when the Northumbrians rebelled against their hated earl, Tostig. King Edward the Confessor accepted Tostig's banishment and appointed the rebels' choice, Morcar, in his place. Soon the Confessor would be dead, Tostig would be fighting his own brother Harold at Stamford Bridge, and Duke William, later known as 'the Conqueror', would arrive from Normandy.

Domesday

What happened at Oxford immediately after the Norman conquest isn't known – but it can't have been pleasant. William sent out teams of tax inspectors to report on the value of land and livestock throughout his new kingdom, and the so-called Domesday Book of 1086 compared their findings with the state of affairs that had existed 20 years before.

Oxford had been devastated.

This is an unsolved mystery. By 1066 the town had spread beyond its Saxon walls to become one of the largest in England, with around 1,000 houses and up to 11 churches, yet 20 years later we find more than half of those houses described as 'waste'. The Normans always responded ferociously to rebellion, but there's no record of any uprising here.

Oxford was granted to one of William's trusted barons, Robert d'Oyly, and within five years of the conquest he began to build a wooden motte-and-bailey castle outside the west gate of the Saxon burh, diverting a side stream of the Thames to create a moat.

Castle fragments

Oxford Castle was 'one of the ruins that Cromwell knocked about a bit', and all that survives today is the mound, St George's Tower and the crypt. They form part of the award-winning Oxford Castle Quarter, which includes a boutique hotel (in the former HM prison), an art gallery and a variety of bars and eateries. The visitor attraction Oxford Castle Unlocked offers daily tours: 'Tales of Murder, Romance, Betrayal and Execution'.

This was later replaced by a stone fortress, the ten-sided shell keep on its mound probably designed as much to cow the locals as to deter would-be attackers. But the Normans characteristically leavened their brutality with piety: St George's Tower, built as early as 1074, included a large chapel (nave, chancel, apsidal sanctuary, crypt) endowed with a college of priests.

Anarchy

The castle faced its first serious test in 1142 during the civil war known as the Anarchy, between Matilda, daughter of the Conqueror's son Henry I, and Stephen, son of the Conqueror's daughter, Adela. (Please concentrate!) This began with Henry's death in 1135 and lasted for some 20 years.

Most of the nobles who had promised to accept Matilda as queen switched sides to Stephen. D'Oyly not only championed her cause but entertained her in Oxford – and he surely can't have been too surprised to see Stephen's army marching up to his castle walls and camping outside.

Stephen broke into the town and burned it, laying seige to the castle for three months. Matilda escaped through a snowy landscape – let down from the walls on a rope (or so the story goes) and crossing the iced-up river at night. D'Oyly then surrendered.

The Anarchy ended at Oxford in 1154, when Stephen met Matilda's son, the future Henry II, and agreed that he should be his successor.

fit for a king

A stone set into a pillar in Beaumont Street commemorates Henry I's Beaumont Palace, built outside the north gate around 1130 and orginally known prosaically as 'the King's Houses'. Two of Henry II's sons, the future kings Richard I and John, were born here.

Richard spent most of his time abroad, but John was often in residence during his reign, and he met the rebellious barons at Oxford in the Magna Carta year of 1215.

Edward II gave the palace to the Carmelites in gratitude for surviving the Battle of Bannockburn in 1314. It was dismantled at the Dissolution, some of the stone being used to enlarge the library of St John's College.

Revolting barons

The town had a last medieval fling at the forefront of national affairs during the Barons' Revolt against Henry III, led by Simon de Montfort.

- In 1258 The Provisions of Oxford were drawn up at the Dominican friary in St Ebbe's parish – echoing Magna Carta some 40 years earlier and claimed as England's first written constitution. Power was to be shared between the king and the barons.

- In March 1264, having reneged on the deal (with the Pope's blessing), Henry summoned the whole knight service of England to Oxford to take the field against 'the king's enemies'. For a time the town was the unofficial military and political capital of England.

- In May 1264 Henry was defeated at the Battle of Lewes, in Sussex. He was forced to sign a document granting new powers to the barons – and was then brought back to Oxford.

- In 1266, de Montfort having been killed the previous year, Henry was in charge at Oxford again – and the townsmen had to pay large fines for having sided with the enemy.

The best of times …

By the middle of the 13th century Oxford was among the leading towns in England, its prosperity based chiefly on cloth and leather. Its first known royal charter, granted around 1155, confirmed liberties, trading privileges and various legal rights which its burgesses had enjoyed since the reign of Henry I.

True, the town had to pay an annual 'fee farm' to the crown for these favours, but in good times the burgesses must have regarded it as an attractive deal. They organised a system of powerful merchant guilds (nobody could pursue a trade or craft without belonging to one), elected a mayor, aldermen and bailiffs and – from 1268 – sent two MPs to Parliament.

Other people enjoyed special concessions, too. St Frideswide's Priory, for instance, was given the right to hold a lucrative fair in the town and to charge tolls for passage over the Thames, while the growing university steadily acquired its own (fiercely resented) privileges – as we shall discover later.

... and the worst

The 14th century, by contrast, was a wretched one for Oxford, and various reasons have been put forward for its sorry decline:

- The guilds were so restrictive in their practices that many craftsmen went elsewhere.
- There was competition from new towns such as Abingdon and Henley further downriver.
- The domination of religious houses soaked up more than 60 per cent of total rent income.
- The 'great famine' of 1315–1317, caused by bad spring weather, brought about calamitous crop failures across all of northern Europe.

Underground history

Many medieval houses were timber-framed with wattle-and-daub walls and thatched roofs, but stone was increasingly used from the mid-12th century as the town grew more prosperous.

The Grade II* listed Mitre Hotel in the High Street (owned by Lincoln College) dates from around 1630, but its 13th-century vaults are the oldest surviving stone cellars in Oxford.

But deadliest of all were the death-dealing bites of engorged fleas given a lift into Oxford in the fur of obliging rats. They arrived in late 1348, delivering a vile affliction known variously as the pestilence, the murrain, the great plague or the Black Death.

Probably between a third and a half of the population perished. Victims died in a feverish delirium, their bodies disfigured by rashes and little black swellings called buboes.

Isabella and Mortimer

In October 1326 national politics forced themselves on Oxford in the guise of the rebel army led by Roger Mortimer, 1st Earl of March, and his mistress Isabella – wife of the weak king Edward II, loathed by many for promoting his homosexual favourites.

The pair heard an inflammatory sermon by the bishop of Hereford, Adam Orleton, in favour of the king's removal. Edward fled London that very day, was desposed the following January and would die (perhaps murdered) within months. Mortimer, deposed in turn by the king's young son, Edward III, was hanged at Tyburn in 1330 – but Queen Isabella survived unscathed.

Holy Oxford

During its medieval heyday Oxford was awash with religious foundations. A survey of 1279, when it's estimated that there were some 1,400 properties in the town, found that ecclesiastical landlords owned, or received rents from, more than 500 of them. (The university, by contrast, held only six schools and a dozen other buildings.)

Small friaries abounded, but the three wealthiest monastic houses at this time were St Frideswide's, refounded as an Augustinian priory in 1122; Osney Abbey, also Augustinian and established in 1129 on an island outside the west gate (it acquired the collegiate church of St George in the Castle in 1149); and Godstow Nunnery, founded in 1133, 2½ miles (4 km) to the northwest, but with considerable land in and around Oxford itself.

A year after the survey, a new house appeared on the scene: the Cistercian Rewley Abbey, endowed by a grandson of King John.

Most of the buildings were slighted (made uninhabitable) in the Dissolution, although Osney enjoyed six years as Oxford's cathedral before that honour passed to Frideswide's church – which had now become part of the new foundation of Christ Church – in 1545.

We have no overall figures for Black Death victims in Oxford, so must look for clues where we can find them. Between April and December 1349, for instance, half the incumbents of the town's 14 parish churches were replaced, at least five of the vacancies caused by death.

Between November 1348 and June 1349 no fewer than 57 wills were lodged in the town register, whereas the normal figure was no more than four during a whole year. These were the wills of the well-to-do who owned property – the dead included two Oxford mayors, Richard Selwood and Richard Cary – and the record shows that ten wills were made in the January, rising to a peak of 16 in April and falling away to two by June.

The death rate was probably higher in more crowded, insanitary areas, but the plague also carried off the abbess of Godstow, the prioress of the Benedictine house at Littlemore, two chancellors of the university and two provosts of Oriel College. Out in the countryside small villages virtually emptied, and some were abandoned for ever.

Oxford must have appeared something of a ghost town after these cumulative blows. In terms of taxable wealth the town had ranked eighth among English provincial towns in 1334, but it had slipped to 14th by the 1370s, when locals welcomed the founding of New College because the area was littered with filth and corpses and was a haunt of criminals and prostitutes. By 1524 the town had fallen to 29th in the ratings – having just been struck by another epidemic altogether.

from king to kitchen boy

After Richard III's death at Bosworth Field in 1485, the Yorkists sought a successor with better claims to the throne than Henry VII, who had deposed him. They hit on the ruse of claiming that Lambert Simnel, the 10-year-old son of an Oxford joiner, was the escaped Earl of Warwick – one of the 'Little Princes in the Tower' whom Richard had probably murdered. An Oxford priest gave the boy a crash course in courtly etiquette.

Simnel was crowned in Dublin in May 1487, but his ragtag army was easily defeated. Henry took pity on the ill-used lad and gave him a job in the royal kitchen as a spit-turner. Though destined never to fly high, he later became a falconer.

Gates and Bastions

The tower of St Michael at the North Gate in Cornmarket is the oldest building in Oxford, dating from around AD 1000, but the surviving fragments of the medieval town wall date from the first half of the 13th century when the original fortifications were overhauled. It ran for about 2 miles (3.2 km), with at least 21 semicircular bastions.

Let's briefly survey what remains, starting from the castle:

West wall (main gate: unknown)
A long stretch of (reduced) wall in Bulwarks Lane, south of George Street, runs northeast towards New Inn Hall Street.

North wall (main gate: Cornmarket Street)
At its western end the boundary line lies on the north side of St Michael's Street, continuing between the buildings on the north side of Ship Street and the south side of Broad Street.

Part of the wall can be seen behind no. 20 St Michael's Street. There are bastions behind nos. 1 and 15 Ship Street, and lengths of wall behind no. 22 Broad Street.

The minor Smith Gate stood at the end of Catte Street, and Hertford College's Octagon was formerly the Lady Chapel, created (perhaps in the 16th century) from a bastion projecting from the town wall.

From here as far as the east gate (which straddled today's High Street) the wall was double in construction. A tall section of it stands in the courtyard of the Turf Tavern, approached via Hell Passage (now St Helens Passage) between Holywell Street and New College Lane, near Hertford College's Bridge of Sighs.

The most impressive section of the wall – a full one-twelfth of it, including five bastions and a sentry walk – survives intact at New College, which has fulfilled its 1379 promise 'to keep in reparation so much of the north and east wall of the said town that should include the said college'. A pierced bastion gives access to the Slype, where the moat ran.

East Wall (main gate: High Street)
The New College wall turns south along Longwall Street to form the beginning of the east wall. It reappears at the back of St Edmund Hall. It then continued behind the east side of Merton Street.

South wall (main gate: St Aldate's)
The sharp bend at Deadman's Walk in Christ Church Meadow marks the spot where the east and south walls met. The south wall survives as the boundary of Merton, Corpus Christi – where there's a bastion – and Christ Church.

Across St Aldate's (where the south gate once stood) the wall picks up on the north side of Brewer Street, forming the boundary with Pembroke College.

fatal glow

The six outbreaks of sweating sickness in England between 1485 and 1551 are among the mysteries of the medical world. The virulent disease rarely spread beyond our shores – it was therefore known as the *sudor anglicus* or 'English sweat' – and each time it paid a swift spring and summer visit, leaving large numbers of sudden deaths in its wake. Then it disappeared for ever.

Victims first shivered with cold, then sweated profusely with pains in their limbs. Some fell dead on the spot after feeling ill for less than an hour. If they were still alive after 24 hours (Ann Boleyn was one such lucky survivor) they could expect to make a full recovery.

Oxford was first affected in 1508, when Thomas More alerted Cardinal Wolsey to 'the severe depredations of the sweating sickness among the young gentlemen of Oxford and Cambridge', but the worst epidemic seems to have been in 1517. Some accounts, perhaps exaggerated, speak of half the population succumbing to it.

Out on their ears

By the middle of Henry VIII's reign Oxford looked inwards rather than to the outside world. Manufacturing had declined, and its craftsmen and traders were chiefly dependent on supplying the growing university. Within this settled little world the monastic piles sat contented upon their great wealth. And then everything changed...

Robert King, the abbot of Osney, was luckier than most when Henry grabbed vast ecclesiastical assets in his Dissolution of the Monasteries. The abbey was spared demolition by being designated a cathedral, and King found himself bishop of Thame and Osney.

Better was to come. The disgraced Cardinal Wolsey had suppressed St Frideswide's Priory with the intention of founding his own grandiose Cardinal College on the site, but Henry now took it over, renamed it Christ Church and, in 1545, made its chapel the cathedral of a new diocese. Osney was allowed to crumble into a ruin, while Robert King was now the very first bishop of Oxford.

Henry had grand plans for his new foundation, but died soon after the work began. The five western bays of the priory church were demolished in order to create the main quadrangle – now Tom Quad – and the rest was supposed to follow suit, with a new chapel built on the north side. In the event the remaining portion of the church survived, becoming a unique two-in-one: both the chapel of the new college and the cathedral of the new diocese.

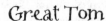

Great Tom

Tom Tower at Christ Church (it is never called 'Christ Church College') was designed by Christopher Wren in 1681, but its bell, Great Tom, is much older. The monks evicted from Osney Abbey in the 1540s would surely have been gratified to know that their bell – reputedly the loudest in Oxford – can still be heard throughout the city in the 21st century.

Two curiosities: the bell is rung 101 times each evening to signify the college's original 100 scholars plus one; and, as the traditional signal to Oxford colleges to close their gates, it chimes at five past nine – local time being five minutes behind Greenwich Mean Time.

Burning issues

The flames of religious discord fanned by Henry VIII became literal funeral pyres during the five-year reign of his Roman Catholic daughter, who earned herself the soubriquet Bloody Mary.

Only three of her 300 Protestant victims died at Oxford, but they were the most famous of all: Thomas Cranmer, the archbishop of Canterbury; Hugh Latimer, a former bishop of Worcester who had been Church of England chaplain to the young Edward VI, Mary's half-brother; and Nicholas Ridley, the bishop of London.

They had no local connections – in fact all three had had the misfortune to be educated at Cambridge – but in 1555 they were conveyed from the Tower of London to Oxford, where they were held in the Bocardo gaol adjoining the church of St Michael at the North Gate. Tried for heresy at the university church of St Mary the Virgin in the High Street, they were sentenced to death by burning.

Latimer and Ridley perished together that October, with Cranmer (given time to repent) obliged to observe their agonies. Five months later he followed them to the stake at the same spot – in the ditch outside the city wall opposite Balliol College.

The city bailiffs put in an expenses claim to the archbishop of Canterbury for dealing with their illustrious guests. Their outlay on Cranmer included the purchase of wine, figs, veal and oysters, charges for a barber and laundry – and the cost of 150 faggots of wood and furze for his bonfire.

Today there are memorials: cobbles in the form of a cross set into the road outside Balliol; the Victorian Martyrs' Memorial round the corner in St Giles; and the door of their cell on display in the tower of St Michael at the North Gate.

Elizabeth's reign was less bloody, but a plaque in the wall at 100 Holywell Street commemorates four Catholics executed in 1589: two of them priests, the others accused of harbouring them.

There's another plaque at Oxford Castle to George Napier, a local man working as a Catholic missionary a generation later. He was hanged, drawn and quartered in 1610, having been found carrying priestly paraphernalia, including holy oils, two consecrated hosts and a small reliquary. It was his bad luck, perhaps, to be caught at a time when the Gunpowder Plot was still fresh in everyone's minds.

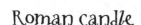

Roman candle

In the Ashmolean Museum you'll come across the lamp carried by Guy Fawkes when he and his fellow Catholic plotters attempted to blow up the Houses of Parliament on 5 November 1605.

It was given to the university in 1641 by Robert Heywood, son of a justice of the peace who was present at Fawkes's arrest in the cellars.

Made of sheet iron, with a candleholder inside, it has a hinged door that was once fitted with a horn window. A vent at the top could be rotated in order to conceal the light.

Some 17th-century highlights

1602 The **Bodleian Library** opens, with an initial stock of 2,000 volumes. Its founder, Thomas Bodley, was a Magdalen scholar and later lecturer in Greek at Merton (he's buried beneath its chapel choir), who came back to Oxford after a diplomatic career. The Bodleian incorporates the 15th-century Duke Humfrey's Library, restored by Bodley after it had been gutted during the Reformation.

1621 Sir Henry Danvers, first earl of Danby, founds the **Oxford University Botanic Garden**, the first in Britain.

1636 Oxford University Press is granted its charter by King Charles I.

1668 Completion of Christopher Wren's **Sheldonian Theatre**, still used today for graduation and degree ceremonies.

1677 Elias Ashmole gives the university his vast 'cabinet of curiosities'. Within six years the collection is housed in the first **Ashmolean Museum** (now the Museum of the History of Science) in Broad Street.

Roundheads and Cavaliers

The next national religio-political furore – the bloody Civil War which set family against family – thrust Oxford into the spotlight for several years. In November 1642 Charles I, facing a growing rebellion throughout the country, attempted to capture London. Forced back by a Parliamentary army, he retreated to Oxford, where his court was to be located for some four years.

The mills at Osney became a powder factory and New College the magazine. Cannon were cast at St Mary's College on the east side of New Inn Hall Street, later rebuilt as Frewin Hall (a gateway remains).

The king was based at Christ Church, the queen at Merton – two gateways were cut to allow them access through the Corpus Christi garden – while the future Charles II and James II had MA degrees conferred upon them, and so did some of their supporters who were billeted in college buildings. Although there was strong Parliamentary sympathy in the town, the university was staunchly Royalist.

The Roundheads laid seige to the castle briefly, and somewhat half-heartedly, in 1644 and again in 1645 – although the gear they assembled for the task on the latter occasion suggests that they initially meant business:

- 2 demi cannons and 3 whole culverins
- 1,200 spades and shovels
- 500 pickaxes
- 300 steel spades
- 200 scaling ladders
- 500 barrels of gunpowder
- 40 tons of match
- 30 tons of bullet
- 300 great grenado shells
- 300 small grenado shells
- 1,000 hand grenades
- 20 carriages for provisions
- 200 horse harness.

They came back again in earnest the following year under Sir Thomas Fairfax, although not in time to prevent Charles slipping through their lines in disguise – with a *montero*, or Spanish hunter's earflapped hat, on his head and a cry of 'Farewell Harry!' from the governor of the castle, Sir Thomas Glemham. As negotiations began for a surrender, Glemham found himself threatened by a mob.

Fairfax delivered his ultimatum on 11 May:

> I do by these summon you to deliver up the City of Oxford into my hands, for the use of Parliament. I very much desire the preservation of that place (so famous for learning) from ruin, which inevitably is like to fall upon it, except you concur. You may have honourable terms for yourself and all within that garrison if you reasonably accept thereof.

In the event it wasn't until 24 June – after delaying tactics by the Oxford garrison and occasional firing of cannon by both sides – that the keys of the city were formally handed over to Fairfax, and more than 2,000 Royalist troops marched away with guarantees of safe conduct in their pockets.

Two of the 59 commissioners who signed the king's death warrant were Oxford born and educated: Henry Marten (University College) and Adrian Scrope (Hart Hall). When Charles II came to the throne in 1660 seeking revenge against the regicides, both were condemned to death. Marten had his sentence commuted to life imprisonment, but Scrope was hanged, drawn and quartered at Charing Cross.

Happy returns

Did Charles II have fond memories of his youthful sojourn at Oxford? Possibly, because when the Great Plague devastated London in 1665 – the worst outbreak since the Black Death more than three centuries earlier, with 7,000 deaths a week recorded that September – it was to Oxford that he took his court to avoid infection. He remained in the city until the following February.

Melted down

During the Royalist occupation the colleges were obliged to melt down much of their plate to make so-called 'Oxford crowns', struck at the mint in New Inn Hall Street to aid Charles I's war effort.

An example can be seen in the Ashmolean Museum. Dated 1644, it depicts the city beneath the king's horse. The inscription on the reverse states that Charles supported the Protestant religion, the laws of England and a free Parliament.

The Royalist stopover gives Oxford a curious place in publishing history: *The London Gazette* – which claims to be the oldest surviving English newspaper and the oldest published continuously in the UK – began life as *The Oxford Gazette* on 7 November 1665. The first appearance of this official record of government business was noted by Samuel Pepys in his famous diary. It changed its name when Charles led his entourage back to the capital, but the first London issue, on 5 February 1666, was labelled no. 24.

Caffeine rush

Reading the papers and discussing politics and literature over a coffee was a mark of civilised life in the second half of the 17th century.

London alone would soon have hundreds of (men-only) coffee houses, but the very first in England was established at Oxford in 1652 by a Jewish businessman named Jacob, at the Angel in the parish of St Peter in the East – and the Grand Café is still serving coffee at the same High Street premises today. Another followed close by in Queen's Lane two years later, and that, too, remains a coffee house.

Some 18th-century highlights

1715 Opening of the **Clarendon Building** in the Broad for the Oxford University Press.

1748 The Grade II* **Holywell Music Room** ('the oldest purpose-built music room in Europe'), opens in Holywell Street. Handel and Haydn both performed here.

1749 The circular, Palladian-style **Radcliffe Camera** is completed to house the science library bequeathed by John Radcliffe (1652–1714), physician to William III and Mary II. The library later moved, allowing the Camera to furnish extra reading rooms for the Bodleian.

1774 The **covered market** opens north of the High Street. Designed by John Gwynn, it at first housed 20 butchers' shops, but soon diversified to include fish, dairy produce and vegetables – and it's still thriving today.

1790 Completion of the 78-mile (125-km) **Oxford Canal**, running to Coventry via Banbury and Rugby. Fifteen years later the Grand Union Canal took away much of the trade, but it remained profitable until the mid-1950s.

After the passions of the Civil War and the Restoration, Oxford settled down to more than a century of comfortable stagnation as a moderately sized market town. Its population in the 1770s was little more than 10,000, it had no manufacturing industry and its small traders and craftsmen largely served the university – and had to budget for the many months when the students were away.

What Oxford did have, from 1771, was a Paving Commission charged not only with sprucing up the streets but improving the townscape as a whole. It set about its work enthusiastically, demolishing the east and north gates (along with the Bocardo prison), replacing street stalls with a new covered market and even shifting house frontages to allow road widening. The new paving of the High Street (large square blocks with side gutters) was regarded as the equal of anything in London.

King corn

The shortages caused by the Napoleonic wars at the beginning of the 19th century brought misery to the Oxford poor, and the city and university joined forces to provide them with cheap, sometimes free, food and coal.

This didn't prevent occasional violence, as the Corn Laws banned imports and so forced up the price of bread. The local militia was called out to deal with rioting mobs, and in 1814 the local MP, John Lockhard, took the precaution of entering the city armed after he had voted against the import of corn.

Can't pay, won't pay

By tradition, a tradesman owed money by a feckless student had one last chance of getting it back. He was allowed to attend the degree ceremony in the Sheldonian Theatre and veto the award by twitching the proctor's cloak when the miscreant's name was called out. The risk was that all the other students might boycott his services in revenge.

Cholera

Civic pride was, however, dealt a dreadful blow in 1832 when the first of three cholera epidemics ravaged the city, laying low 184 people and claiming the lives of 95 of them.

By this time the population had risen to over 20,000, and many families were living in slum conditions, especially in the growing suburbs. The St Clement's, St Ebbe's, St Thomas's and Jericho areas were the worst affected.

The reasons for the rapid spread of the outbreak weren't hard to find: drainage was inadequate throughout the city – there were countless cesspools and vile privies in areas liable to flood – while the outfall from five sewers discharged into the Thames above the (unfiltered) waterworks, and the city centre churchyards were filled to overflowing.

What Oxford needed now was a dose of Victorian drive and public-spiritedness. What it also needed was a consensus between the local authorities and the university – and history wasn't encouraging on that score…

Oxford waterways

The Oxford Canal meets the Thames just north
of the city centre. The canal now ends at Hythe
Bridge Street; originally it passed under the
bridge and its wharves extended to where
Nuffield College now stands.

CHAPTER TWO

TOWN AND GOWN

A royal charter gave the inhabitants of medieval towns precious rights and freedoms that must have been the envy of country cousins forced to obey the lord of the manor's every whim. Within their stone walls they were licensed to run their own business and social affairs much as they wished.

For the burgesses of Oxford, alas, life was never quite so comfortable. They had a cuckoo in their nest – a noisy, restless intruder that would never fly away.

The university first began to flourish in the late 12th century, and from the beginning there seems to have been friction between townsfolk and tonsured students. (All scholars were enrolled in the church as clerks in minor orders, and dressed rather like monks.)

In 1209 we find the first recorded clash ending with loss of life: two or three students were accused of murder and hanged. But if this was a victory for the townsmen – many students fled in terror, and the university was temporarily closed down – it was to be a short-lived one.

King John's quarrel with Pope Innocent III had led to his being excommunicated, but the two settled their differences in 1213, and in the following year a papal legate arrived in Oxford to impose severe financial penalties on the town – and to enforce various indignities besides:

• Those responsible for the hangings were to do penance by marching in procession to their victims' graves, barefoot and coatless, followed by the entire populace of the town.

- For ten years half the rent of existing hostels and schools was to be cancelled, and after that period rents would be fixed at the previous rate for a further ten years.

- The townsmen were to pay an annual sum, in perpetuity, which would be distributed among poor students on the feast of St Nicholas (the patron saint of scholars), and on that day they must also provide 100 poor scholars with bread and beer, pottage and flesh or fish.

- Any clerk arrested by the townsmen must be immediately surrendered to the Bishop of Lincoln (in whose diocese Oxford lay), 'or the Archdeacon of the place, or his official or the Chancellor or whomsoever the Bishop of Lincoln shall depute to this office'.

- The mayor, bailiffs and up to 50 burgesses ('as many as the Bishop should require') were to take an oath every year, publicly honouring the settlement, and so adding further humiliation to what was already a shaming agreement.

No doubt much of the trouble had been caused by unruly, drink-fuelled young men on the rampage, disturbing the peace of the town – not all scholars were at their books from morn till night.

From this point onwards, however, the local people would have the further grievance of knowing that the rights and privileges of the masters and pupils in their midst would steadily increase while their own diminished.

In 1240 Bishop Grosseteste (who had taught at the university) created a charitable institution to administer the funds accruing from the legate's annual fine a generation earlier.

At that time Jews were the only licensed moneylenders, and they were charging local scholars interest of more than 40 per cent a year. Under the new scheme the money was lodged in a chest at St Frideswide's Priory for the benefit of poor scholars. In pawnbroker fashion, a borrower would place inside it an item – a book, perhaps, a cup or an item of clothing – whose value exceeded the amount of the loan. Any unredeemed pledges were sold by public auction at the end of a year.

The fund was later augmented by private bequests – the donors asking only that, in return for their generosity, the recipient should say prayers for their souls.

The Jewish connection

Oxford's medieval Jewish quarter lay on either side of St Aldate's, with a synagogue on the east side of the street (where the northwest tower of Christ Church now stands) and a burial ground outside the east gate.

Jews enjoyed privileges from the monarch in return for bolstering the royal finances, and the first written record of the local community dates from 1141 when Queen Matilda was besieged in the castle. She apparently extracted gold from the Jews before making her escape (see page 30). When Stephen in turn demanded money, they told him there wasn't much left – whereupon he set fire to their largest house, at the southeast corner of Carfax, and threatened to burn down the rest.

Many leading Oxford Jews were ruined by the financial exactions of King John, and when in 1279 some were hanged for coin-clipping (trimming the edges of coins to steal their precious metal), only a few families remained.

All Jews in England were expelled by Edward I in 1290, and there wouldn't be another community in the town until Oliver Cromwell invited them back in 1656.

61

Some 13th-century lowlights

1228 After townsmen attacked and wounded scholars, the town was placed under an interdict.

1232 A future mayor, Adam Fettiplace, was among seven men imprisoned for injuring clerks.

1236 Amid more disturbances, the town was set on fire – deliberately, it was presumed.

1238 No townsmen were involved this time, but rioting students assaulted the papal legate (who escaped with his life) and his brother (who didn't). This time the university was placed under an interdict, and scholars – forbidden to leave the town – were forced to find sureties for their good behaviour.

1248 After yet another student was killed, Henry III briefly took the town into his own hands.

1249 Neither side gave up fighting for Lent, when there was an orgy of violence and looting.

1264–1266 After a series of riots, during which the townsmen labelled students 'foreigners' and the students divided themselves into Northerners and Southerners, some students were hanged and others imprisoned. The king dispatched justices to sort things out.

The king gets tough

It was bad enough for the Pope to throw his weight about, but further outbreaks of violence proved too much for the king himself to bear. Henry III's interventions seem always to have been to the university's advantage.

• After the 1248 brutality it was ruled that if a townsman killed or wounded a clerk the community as a whole was to be fined, with the bailiffs being punished separately if they were held to have been negligent.

• Four years later there was a legal victory for the university, giving clerks immunity from civil action. The chancellor of the university had the right to try and punish them for all offences except *atrocia crimina* – murder, in short.

• In 1255 Henry reorganised the town's government in an attempt to rid it of its continued lawlessness. Under a new law, a layman who injured a clerk was to be gaoled until he paid compensation, whereas a clerk who injured a layman was simply to be handed over to the chancellor.

The chancellor's court was an ecclesiastical one, and it had a very wide remit. It could rule on disputes involving clerks in matters of tax, house rentals and commercial contracts. From 1260 it was given jurisdiction over actions between individual scholars and Jews, and in 1275 students were granted the right to cite burgesses before the chancellor.

As for the perennial problem of student accommodation, the university won a deal for rents to be frozen for five-year periods, much to the landlords' disgust.

Northampton rusticated

In 1261 Henry III granted a charter to the University of Northampton, the first to be established in England after Oxford and Cambridge. Unluckily for its first dons and scholars, the king was petitioned by a group of bishops and magnates who warned that its existence would damage Oxford. In 1265 Henry issued a royal decree which dissolved it.

The town had to wait another 840 years. In 2005 University College Northampton was upgraded to university status and given the name of its short-lived ancestor.

After another outbreak of fighting in 1290 a new agreement imposed a few rare restraints on the chancellor – he had, for instance, to give townsmen a day's notice to appear in his court, rather than an hour, and he wasn't allowed to release a clerk imprisoned for seriously wounding a layman until it was known whether or not his victim would live. It was clear, though, that he was still top dog.

A list was drawn up of what would become known as 'privileged persons' – those entitled to share the special rights of the university. They included clerks and their families and servants, parchment makers, limners (painters of illuminated manuscripts), scriveners (scribes or notaries), barbers and others who wore clerks' livery.

The chancellor predictably came out on top again after a notable riot in 1298. Certain townsmen were forbidden to have any dealings at all with the university, others were expelled from the town, and the bailiffs were removed and debarred from holding the office in future. The mayor, aldermen and bailiffs swore yet again to preserve the university's privileges.

Among the greatest insults to local people were the regulations that hit them in their pockets. One of the provisions of the 1248 settlement gave the chancellor a say in the quality and price of bread, ale and wine. Subsequent rulings would give the university an ever greater control of the markets.

The St Scholastica's Day riot

The daddy of all riots began on 10 February 1355, the memorial day of St Scholastica. It lasted for three days, and had a consequence that would reverberate for centuries.

Two students, Walter Spryngeheuse and Roger de Chesterfield, accused mine host of the Swyndelstock Tavern at Carfax, John Croidon, of serving them substandard wine. Croidon complained to the mayor that the young men had thrown the wine at him and then hit him on the head with a quart pot.

Some 200 scholars then resisted the bailiffs' attempt to arrest the clerks, assaulting the mayor and other townsmen. In the mêlée a child of 14 was killed.

Battle lines were now drawn. The municipal records claim that on the second day of the conflict the students sealed the gates of the town, ransacked buildings and robbed and wounded large numbers of people. The university version of events was that around 80 townsmen launched an uprovoked attack with bows and arrows on scholars walking in Beaumont Fields.

During that afternoon a large contingent of countrymen – one account says 2,000 of them – entered the town in support of the citizens, reportedly crying 'Slay, slay, havok, havok, smite fast, give good knocks!'

Over the next 36 hours some 20 university halls of residence were destroyed and several scholars (some accounts say as many as 63) were hunted and killed. Many townsmen perished, too, before it was over.

A bank now stands on the site of the tavern where the trouble started, and there's a memorial plaque on the wall.

Chaucer's Oxford scholars

The Oxford scholar who rides with the other pilgrims in Geoffrey Chaucer's late 14th-century *Canterbury Tales* would surely have kept well away from unseemly riots in the town:

A clerk there was of Oxenford also,
Who'd immersed himself in logic long ago.
His wretched horse was thinner than a rake,
And he himself a match, I undertake,
With features gaunt and countenance austere,
The coat above his waist well nigh threadbare,
For as yet he'd no church living to enjoy,
Nor, worldly, stooped to find himself employ.
He'd rather stock the table by his bed
With twenty volumes bound in black and red
Of Aristotle's deep philosophy
Than rich robes, violin or psaltery.
Despite his philosophical career,
He had no stone for making gold appear;
But everything he borrowed from his friends
He spent on books for intellectual ends,
And prayed with passion for the souls of all
Who furnished him with learning's wherewithal.
Study, then, took all his time and care.
His conversation, reticent and spare,
Was formal, showed respect and, all the while,
Short and to the point, of lofty style.
Steeped in moral virtue was his speech,
And gladly would he learn, and gladly teach.

The story told by the clerk is less well known than the Miller's Tale, whose 'hero' is another Oxford clerk, but cut from very different cloth.

Nicholas, who studies astrology and is a fine musician, is also a lusty young blood. He boards with an elderly carpenter and his beautiful 18-year-old wife. While the carpenter is away at Osney (Chaucer clearly knew his Oxford: the old man at one point invokes St Frideswide), Nicholas seduces her, and the two plan a night of passion together. Tricking the old man will be easy, he says, for an Oxford scholar:

> A clerk has misapplied his time, alas,
> If he can't make a carpenter an ass.

The trick works, but has unforeseen consequences. A parish clerk named Absolom also lusts after the young wife, and he calls out to her from under her window, asking for a kiss – not realising that Nicholas is with her.

In the dark she puts her backside out of the window. When he realises what he has kissed, he returns to take his revenge with a red-hot poker. This time Nicholas proffers his rump, loudly farts in Absolom's face – and is agonisingly singed. Too clever by half!

Once the dust had settled, both the town and the university were ordered to surrender their charters pending a new deal between the two sides. The eventual outcome, as always, was severe for the townsmen. Some of their leaders were imprisoned in the Tower of London – and that was only the start of it.

In addition, 63 citizens (one for each student killed) were obliged to attend Mass at the University Church every St Scholastica's Day thereafter, to swear an oath and to pay a silver penny each – a perpetual humiliation. (It speaks volumes for English subservience to tradition that it wasn't until 1800 that a mayor refused to comply with this annual ritual – and was then fined for his temerity; that in 1803 the university refused to accept the tribute in copper rather than silver; that it reluctantly agreed to abolish the coin-giving in 1825, while still demanding the mayor's oath; and that the oath itself was at last allowed to lapse in 1860 only after rancorous debate.)

Worst of all, when the town received its new charter, it found that many of its crucial ancient liberties had passed to the university:

- control of the assize of bread and ale, and of weights and measures

- the power of enquiry into market-riggers and sellers of bad meat or fish

- the punishment of anyone found carrying arms in the town

- the keeping clean of courts and streets

- the taxing and assessing of scholars' servants.

This decisive shift in the balance of power would embitter relations between town and gown for centuries to come.

'There is probably not a single yard in any part of the classic High Street between St Martin's and St Mary's which has not, at one time or another, been stained with blood. There are historic battlefields where less has been spilt.'

Philosopher Hastings Rashdall (1858–1924)

Still at it

Cuthbert M. Bede's humorous novel *The Adventures of Mr Verdant Green*, published in the 1850s, involves its eponymous young Oxford graduate in a bloody town and gown confrontation some 500 years after the St Scholastica's Day riot:

The Town had separated into two or three portions, which had betaken themselves to the most probable fighting points, and had gone where glory waited them, thirsting for the blood, or, at any rate, for the bloody noses of the gowned aristocrats.

Woe betide the luckless gownsman, who, on such an occasion, ventures abroad without an escort, or trusts to his own unassisted powers to defend himself! He is forthwith pounced upon by some score of valiant Townsmen, who are on the watch for these favourable opportunities for a display of their personal prowess, and he may consider himself very fortunate if he is able to get back to his College with nothing worse than black eyes and bruises.

It is so seldom that the members of the Oxford snobocracy have the privilege afforded them of using their fists on the faces and persons of the members of the Oxford aristocracy, that when they do get the chance, they are unwilling to let it slip through their fingers.

The fact that riots were less frequent during the later Middle Ages perhaps reflects the diminished state of both university and town after the Black Death, but the records show continual sparring between the two sides.

A settlement of 1458 (after a renewed bout of fighting), gave a list of those now regarded as 'privileged persons' under the chancellor's protection:

> Doctors, masters, graduates, students, scholars, and clerks living within the precincts of the university and their daily servants; the steward and 'feed men' of the university with their menials; bedels with their daily servants and households; stationers, bookbinders, limners, scriveners, parchment makers, barbers, the university bell-ringer, with their households; all caters, manciples, spencers [these are all people concerned with the procurement of provisions], cooks, launderers, poor children of scholars or clerks within the university; all servants taking clothing or hire by the year, half year, or quarter at a rate of 6s. 8d. a year from any master, doctor, graduate, scholar, or clerk; and all common carriers, bringers of scholars or their money or letters to or from the university, for the time of their stay within the university.

The university remained jealous of its privileges into the modern era:

- Until as late as 1950 it sent two MPs to Parliament, while the town had only one.
- It retained its right to representation on the City Council until 1974.
- The jurisdiction of the chancellor's court in cases involving university members was, though rarely used, officially abolished only in 1977.

Licking a lord

During the Victorian period a class animus surfaces. In the England of Empire the wealthy and would-be influential sent their sons to the likes of Eton and Harrow, and then on to Oxbridge. University was for the swells. After wild disturbances in 1867, when the military was called in, the *Daily Telegraph* commented:

> Oxford has suburbs, like the one nicknamed Jericho, containing plenty of rough bargees and railway labourers glad to lick a lord, and the young and hot blood of the students regards it as an equal luxury to thrash a cad.

The excuse for rioting, should one be needed, was no longer St Scholastica's Day but Bonfire Night. It's a sign of how bad things *used* to be that in 1879, after 21 arrests had been made on 5 November, the *Oxford Chronicle* felt able to declare that 'town and gown riots have now fortunately become almost a thing of the past'.

That proved to be optimistic – although later outbreaks were puny compared with their medieval forerunners. The great cricketer and all-round sportsman C. B. Fry (Repton School and Wadham), for instance, appeared in court in 1895 for damaging a gas lamp, while all students were banned from political rallies two years later after another Wadham student fired a revolver in the air at one: tame stuff!

The bulldog breed

From 1829 until as recently as 2003 the university had its own police force with powers of arrest – the notorious bowler-hatted, dark-suited 'bulldogs', whose remit extended from the university precincts to within 4 miles (6.5 km) of any university building. They still exist, but are now comparatively toothless.

Bully for them

For outsiders the Bullingdon Club is the epitome of upper-class excess and condescension. Founded as a sporting club in the late 18th century, it's become better known for its well-lubricated dinners and their aftermath – violent rampages for which the well-heeled members are happy to pay damages.

Evelyn Waugh mentions the club by name in *Brideshead Revisited* and calls it the Bollinger in *Decline and Fall*, the hero of which is sent down after being blamed for the club's ransacking of his college.

Members wear a uniform of teal-blue frock coat and mustard waistcoat – the latter a fitting colour, as an initiation rite involves a new member consuming a whole tin of Colman's English mustard before having his room trashed.

In 2013 the *Oxford Student* newspaper reported that a new recruit had earned his membership by burning a £50 note in front of a homeless person. This was later denied – but, true or not, it's just the kind of thing the public expects of the Bullingdon.

Members have included many subsequently famous public figures. King Edward VIII was a member (as Prince of Wales), until Queen Mary found out he'd been at a rowdy session and demanded that he resign.

Historically, as well as pitched battles, there were sometimes athletics events between townsmen and students, and today they compete for some 60 trophies in 40 different sports.

An end to hostilities, then? Not necessarily: the annual Oxford City Stars (town) vs. Oxford University Blues (gown) men's ice-hockey match was suspended after 2004 – and didn't resume until 2012 – because of violent clashes which each side blamed on the other.

It was hardly on the scale of St Scholastica's Day, but, as a Blues spokesman explained, 'We can't afford serious injuries like broken arms or wrists, both of which have occurred in this fixture, just before a Varsity match.'

These days, of course, there are women students to be taken into consideration, too – a state of affairs unimaginable when the first Oxford dons gathered their students about them all those centuries ago.

Street cred

Here's every would-be student's essential guide to university argot.

Short forms: Broad Street, High Street and Turl Street are known as The Broad, The High and The Turl, while the Bodleian Library is The Bod (or Bodley), the Examination Schools are The Schools and the University Parks are The Parks.

University terms: Only eight weeks each, these are Michaelmas (autumn), Hilary (spring) and Trinity (summer).

Pronunciation: *Magdalen* as in 'maudlin'.
Viva (oral exam) rhymes with 'skiver'.
Gaudy (college reunion) rhymes with 'bawdy'.

Aegrotat: A degree awarded to a student too ill to sit the exam. The name is Latin for 'He/she is ill.'

Battels: A college bill, payable at the end of term.

Blue: A sports award (dark blue) for representing the university in a 'varsity' match against (light blue) Cambridge. Half-blues are given for sports regarded as minor.

Buttery: A college shop, selling basic provisions.

Come up: To arrive at the university.

Don: A professor, lecturer or college fellow.

D. Phil.: Doctor of Philosophy – what most other universities call a Ph. D.

Eights Week: Inter-college rowing event in Trinity term (see page 175).

Encaenia (rhymes with 'senior'): Ceremony during Trinity term, at which honorary degrees are awarded.

Go down: To leave the university, either temporarily or permanently.

Greats: Classics.

Long vac: The summer holidays.

Matriculation: Formal admission to the university.

Mods: Exams taken at the end of one's first year (short for 'Honour Moderations').

Porter: Receptionist/security guard at front door of a college.

Proctor: One of two dons elected for a year to oversee university discipline.

Rustication: A disbarment from the university for a serious offence.

Scout: College housekeeper.

Sent down: Ejected from the university.

Sporting one's oak: In a college room with double doors, keeping the outer one closed to show that you don't wish to be disturbed.

Subfusc: Formal dress for matriculation, exams and graduation, worn with a cap and gown. The rigid 'mortarboard' first became popular in the 16th century; women, until recently, wore a soft square cap instead. From August 2012, 'Students identifying as either sex can wear historically male or female clothes.'

Torpids: Inter-college rowing event in Hilary term, less prestigious than Eights Week.

Doctor Mirabilis

Roger Bacon (1214–1294), as imagined
by a 19th-century artist. Early scholars
were invariably in holy orders and had
tonsured heads.

CHAPTER THREE

DREAMING SPIRES

The bad blood between Henry II and his combative archbishop of Canterbury Thomas Becket not only ended with a martyrdom, but had an important academic spin-off, too.

In 1167, with the 'turbulent priest' holed up in France and threatening to excommunicate him, a seriously rankled Henry banned all English students from attending the recently founded university of Paris. At least 50 of them obediently packed their bags – and set up their writing desks at Oxford.

Individual masters were already teaching here – perhaps that's what drew them to the spot – but this sudden influx in numbers is reckoned to mark the first flowering in the English-speaking world of the medieval *studium generale*, or university.

Teaching before the 12th century had chiefly been in the hands of the monastic houses and cathedrals – and their schools had life in them yet – but these new communities of learned masters and far-travelled disciples quickly grew in both size and influence. They had no permanent buildings of their own, and no great wealth, but they enjoyed a degree of bracing intellectual independence.

Welcome, stranger

The first known overseas student at the university was Emo of Friesland. Born at Fivelgo (now in the Netherlands), he came up to Oxford aged about 15, in 1190.

He later became the prior of Bloemhof Abbey in Wittewierum – founded in 1198 – and wrote the first part of its chronicles in a lively, semi-autobiographical style.

The rapid rise in numbers is astonishing. In 1192 the Benedictine monk Richard of Devizes wrote that the place had so many scholars that it could scarcely feed them. When the chronicler Matthew Paris recorded the town–gown troubles of 1209 (see page 58) not long after the event, he claimed that 3,000 students had fled Oxford for Cambridge.

Who were they? Not the sons of the labouring masses, clearly, and not many of them from the higher echelons of society where success in life was already guaranteed. They were chiefly the aspiring sons of the middling classes (yeomen farmers, retainers, citizens of the towns), for whom a liberal education offered a way of rising in the church, or becoming a doctor, a lawyer or a civil servant. They took minor orders – progress was only possible through the church – and, in some cases from the age of 14, became 'poor scholars' at the feet of a master.

What did they learn? The *trivium* (grammar, logic and rhetoric), followed by the *quadrivium* (geometry, arithmetic, astronomy and music – all regarded as branches of mathematics).

Oxford roll-call 1

A congregation of students who have passed through the colleges over the years. This list excludes prime ministers, who are listed separately on pages 118–119.

Balliol
John Wycliffe, John Evelyn, Adam Smith, Cardinal Henry Edward Manning, Matthew Arnold, Gerard Manley Hopkins, Cosmo Lang, Hilaire Belloc, William Beveridge, William Temple, Siegfried Sassoon, Aldous Huxley, Grahame Greene, The Nawab of Pataudi Snr, Laurence Whistler, Denis Healey

Brasenose
John Foxe, Robert Burton, Elias Ashmole, Thomas Traherne, William Webb Ellis, Walter Pater, Field Marshal Earl Haig, John Buchan, William Golding, Rt Revd Robert Runcie, Michael Palin

Christ Church (a.k.a. The House)
Philip Sidney, John Locke, Christopher Wren, Robert Hooke, William Penn, John Wesley, Charles Wesley, John Ruskin, John Taverner (Tudor composer), William Walton, Lewis Carroll, King Edward VII, W. H. Auden

Corpus Christi
John Keble, Thomas Arnold, John Ruskin, Robert Bridges, C. P. Scott, Henry Newbolt, Isaiah Berlin, Max Beloff, Kenneth Dover, William Waldegrave

Exeter

Charles Lyell, R. D. Blackmore, Edward Burne-Jones, Francis Palgrave, William Morris (artist and writer), Hubert Parry, Alfred Noyes, J. R. R. Tolkien, Richard Burton (actor), Roger Bannister, Alan Bennett, Philip Pullman, Martin Amis, Will Self

Hertford (including Hart Hall and Magdalen Hall)

William Tyndale, John Donne, John Selden, William Waller, Jonathan Swift, Thomas Hobbes, Henry Pelham, Charles James Fox, Evelyn Waugh, Gavin Maxwell, Dom Mintoff, Tobias Wolff

Jesus

Henry Vaughan, Beau Nash, T. E. Lawrence, Magnus Magnusson, Dom Moraes, Robert Skidelsky, Paul Jones, Ian Boyd, Francine Stock

Keble

Chad Varah, Geoffrey Hill, Imran Khan, Humphrey Carpenter, Giles Coren, Ed Balls

Lady Margaret Hall

Elizabeth Longford, Rachel Trickett, Mary Warnock, Antonia Fraser, Pauline Neville-Jones, Marina Warner, Eliza Manningham-Buller, Benazir Bhutto, Ann Widdecombe, Nigella Lawson, Michael Gove

Lincoln

Edward Thomas, Theodor 'Dr Seuss' Geisel, Osbert Lancaster, John Le Carré, Tom Paulin

The great scholar Gerald of Wales, later chaplain to King Henry II, taught briefly at Oxford in its early years, dividing his time daily between three groups: poor clerks, academics from various faculties, and knights and similar high-ranking students. His classes were much larger than he could have hoped to attract at one of the local monastic schools.

Tit for tat

The medieval academic pecking order meant that the first three universities to be founded – Salerno, Bologna and Paris – would only accept a master from elsewhere if he had taken one of their exams, whereas their own teachers were universally welcome without question.

After Pope Gregory IX set up the University of Toulouse in 1233 he issued a bull giving its masters the same status, whereupon most other universities queued up for a similar papal blessing. Oxford (along with Padua) refused to bend the knee. It was too important not to be regarded as a *studium generale*, but its masters weren't allowed to teach in Paris without an examination.

The response was unsurprising. Forget that bull: Paris masters weren't allowed into Oxford without passing a test, either. *Touché!*

Under one roof

It was probably the need to curb the excesses of their wild young charges that prompted the authorities to insist that all students live in halls together rather than, dangerously unsupervised, in houses sprinkled around the town. There were soon halls by the hundred.

Not long afterwards, wealthy benefactors began to found colleges with permanent teaching staff, although, until further income furnished scholarships for poor students, these were for graduates only.

Which was the first? It's a three-way tussle for primacy between University College, Balliol and Merton, all established around the middle of the 13th century, and we're not foolish enough to enter the fray. What we *do* note is that Merton's Mob Quad, started in 1288, is the oldest quadrangle in the university, and that the college describes its library – the first books arrived in 1276 – as 'the oldest continuously functioning library for university academics and students in the world'.

Three early scholars

The philosopher and Franciscan friar **Roger Bacon** (1214–1294) came up to Oxford at the age of 13 and later became a master at the university, lecturing on Aristotle and earning the tag Doctor Mirabilis ('Wonderful Teacher').

He's been called 'the father of empiricism' because of the scientific experiments which led some to regard him as a magician and, worse, a person in league with the Devil.

An attractive legend relates that Bacon disguised himself as a workman when learned doctors arrived from Cambridge. He argued against them so devastatingly that they went home believing that in Oxford even humble labourers had better minds than theirs.

'Friar Bacon's Study' stood on Folly Bridge until 1779.

One of the greatest medieval philosopher-theologians, **John Duns Scotus** (1266–1308), was educated at Oxford's Franciscan *studium* – behind St Ebbe's Church – and he seems to have been back in the city around 1300 to take part in a debate.

He was known as Doctor Subtilis ('the Subtle Teacher') because of his finely nuanced thinking (from him we have the word *haecceity*, for the essential 'thisness' of an object or an individual), but later theologians dismissed much of his work as mere word-spinning sophistry.

This led to an unfortunate nickname, which has stuck. In harsher times, poorly performing pupils would be forced to stand in a corner of the classroom wearing a cap with the letter D on it. That stood for 'dunce' – a crude insult to an outstanding mind.

William of Ockham (c. 1288–1348), another Franciscan friar and scholastic philosopher, studied theology at Oxford for a dozen years without taking a degree. He's noted for his 'principle of parsimony', otherwise known as 'Occam's Razor': crudely expressed, it states that the simpler of two competing theories is usually the correct one.

The devastation brought about by the Black Death (see page 34) had an inevitable effect on the student population – the number of halls licensed by the university fell steadily from the 14th to the early 16th centuries – but the dereliction of large areas of the town offered an irresistible opportunity for existing colleges to expand and new ones to spring up.

- From 1317 to 1412 Merton acquired most of the land lying between Merton Street and the town wall.

- Queen's bought the northern part of its site in Queen's Lane between 1341 and 1347 and a frontage on High Street in 1357.

- Oriel first occupied its site in Shidyerd Street (now Oriel Square) between 1329 and 1392.

- University College moved into the High Street in the 1330s.

- Exeter (originally Stapeldon Hall) bought its site in Turl Street around 1336.

- In 1364 St Frideswide's bought nine empty plots near the priory in order to establish the Benedictine Canterbury College.

- New College (see page 37) was built on no fewer than 51 vacant plots accumulated by William of Wykeham between 1370 and 1379.

The rate of growth slowed down during the 15th century, but All Souls sprang up in 1440 on the site of nine tenements in Catte Street and High Street; Lincoln College acquired its Turl Street site between 1430 and 1463; while in 1448 William Waynefleete built his Magdalen Hall on nine tenements and three gardens between High Street and Merton Street. (Ten years later, now Lord Chancellor, he would replace it with the much grander Magdalen College on the site of the St John the Baptist hospital outside the east gate.)

The university itself got in on the development act when, in 1427, it began work on its first major building, the Divinity School – now attached to the Bodleian, with Duke Humfrey's Library above – designed for lectures and seminars on theology.

Oxford itself was far from wealthy, but within little more than a century it had become an imposing town of large stone buildings, grouped around quadrangles (New College had set that example) behind high walls. Its essential character had been established for all time.

Another turbulent priest

John Wycliffe came to Oxford from Yorkshire as a 15-year-old in 1345, became (if briefly) master of Balliol by the age of 30, and was associated with the university for the rest of his life. The university itself, having originally esteemed his work as a philosopher, theologian, teacher and lay preacher, later threw him out because of his dangerous reforming zeal.

His iconoclasm has earned Wycliffe the less than snappy moniker 'the morning star of the Reformation'. He was, to grossly simplify his deep and closely argued treatises:

- against the power of the Pope in secular affairs
- against the wealth of the Church
- against the corruption involved in the selling of indulgences
- against the belief that the real body and blood of Christ were consumed in the Eucharist
- for the secularisation of ecclesiastic properties
- for a ministry of poor priests
- for the authority of the Bible as the word of God.

Putting these tenets into practice, he sent itinerant preachers around the country in pairs, barefoot, wearing long dark-red robes and carrying staffs which symbolised their pastoral calling. Called 'Lollards' ('mumblers') by their detractors, they accepted the derogatory term as a badge of honour.

He also produced the very first Bible in the English language, translating it from the Latin Vulgate – and possibly supplying all of the New Testament books himself. The first version appeared in 1382, several further editions were issued in later years, and more than 250 manuscripts survive today.

Wycliffe was perhaps lucky in his timing: in the more vicious period that followed, he might have ended his life on a bonfire. As it was, he died in his bed on the last day of 1384, and when he was officiallly declared a heretic by the Council of Constance in 1415 the flames consumed only his books and his remains – dug up and cremated on the orders of the Pope. His ashes were scattered in the River Swift at Lutterworth, Leicestershire, his last home.

from Hart Hall to Hertford

The piecemeal development of the early colleges and the fluctuating fortunes of the university over the centuries are epitomised by the highs and lows in the story of Hertford College.

- Hart Hall is founded in Catte Street by Elias de Hertford during the 1280s as a boarding house for undergraduates.

- In 1312 it passes to Bishop Walter de Stapledon, the founder of Exeter College, and is used by the fellows of Exeter for teaching purposes.

- By the early 16th century it has absorbed its immediate neighbours, Black Hall (where John Wycliffe was once held under arrest) and Cat Hall.

- Under its principal Philip Rondell (1548–1599), a man with strong Catholic leanings, the hall becomes independent of Exeter and acquires new buildings. John Donne is one of its scholars.

- After the Civil War, numbers are so low that Oliver Cromwell has to step in to appoint a new principal.

- The hall recovers after the Restoration, but the building of a new gateway with library above pitches it into debt.

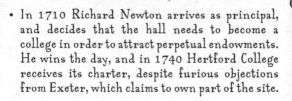

- In 1710 Richard Newton arrives as principal, and decides that the hall needs to become a college in order to attract perpetual endowments. He wins the day, and in 1740 Hertford College receives its charter, despite furious objections from Exeter, which claims to own part of the site.

- By 1805 it's clear that the fellows have been over-ambitious. No-one can be found to replace the principal, and the college is dissolved. In 1820 its medieval façade collapses into Catte Street.

- In 1816 Magadalen College buys the site on behalf of Magdalen Hall (see page 91), which builds two new wings and brings with it a renowned library.

- The hall is re-established as Hertford College in 1874, when the principal attracts substantial support from the financier Thomas Baring.

- New quads, and the famous 'Bridge of Sighs' over the entrance to New College Lane, complete the complex during the late 19th and early 20th centuries.

Some of Wycliffe's followers were not so lucky. In 1401 the first English statute was passed for the burning of heretics, and many of them were to suffer that grisly fate. Being found with the vernacular Bible was condemnation enough. In 1408 the English clergy met at Oxford under the archbishop of Canterbury and drew up the Constitutions of Oxford, which outlawed the reading and the translation of the scriptures into English without the permission of the bishop. Lollardy and Wycliffe's Bible were driven underground for more than 100 years.

Change ~ but not too much

When the Renaissance flowered in England, with a rediscovery of ancient art, poetry and philosophy, the university was at its forefront in the person of John Colet, who took his MA at Magdalen, studied abroad for a few years and then, in 1496, returned to teach at Oxford.

Colet drew less on the artistic and pagan aspects of the rediscovered culture than on its moral and religious implications. He lectured on the epistles of St Paul, replacing the dry old scholastic method with an invigorating humanistic interpretation. He invited the great Erasmus to join him, and the Oxford Reformers, as they were known, attacked the extortion of ecclesiastical courts, the worship of relics and images, and the corrupt worldliness of monks and clergy.

The Reformation, on the other hand, was a step too far for the university. We've noted that the so-called Oxford martyrs were in fact all Cambridge men, and that's no coincidence. Luther's Ninety-Five Theses, first published in 1517, were enthusiastically debated at the other place (which would spawn such noted Protestant figures as Coverdale, Cranmer and Latimer), but Oxford covered its ears and opted for orthodoxy.

The university was forced to accept Henry VIII's divorce from Catherine of Aragon, but his takeover of the Church prompted many fellows to leave and take up posts in Catholic Europe. Several ended up at the new University of Douai in Flanders (founded in 1559), which therefore had a distinct Oxford flavour in its early years.

An Oxford saint

Edmund Campion (1540–1581) was Oxford's very own religious martyr. He came up to St John's in 1557, became a junior fellow and was so highly regarded that in 1566 he personally welcomed Queen Elizabeth to Oxford and led a public debate in her presence.

At first a closet Roman Catholic, who took holy orders in the Anglican Church in 'a remorse of conscience and detestation of mind', he later trained as a Jesuit in Rome. In 1580 he joined a mission to England which the Crown regarded as treasonable.

Arriving in the guise of a jewel merchant, he emerged from a series of safe houses to preach to the faithful. His *Ten Reasons*, arguing against the validity of the Anglican church, further inflamed anti-Papist passions; 400 copies were found on the benches of the university church of St Mary the Virgin. After he was captured, in July 1581, he was taken, arms pinioned, to London with 'Campion, the Seditious Jesuit' scrawled on a piece of paper tucked into his hat.

After being tortured on the rack, he was hanged, drawn and quartered at Tyburn on 1 December 1581. Pope Paul VI canonised him in 1970.

Henry's dissolution of the monasteries was bad news for two of the Oxford colleges. **Canterbury College**, owned by the priory in the Kent city, had originally appointed John Wycliffe as its warden, but, after a row which involved the Curia in Rome, the education was confined to monks – with a monk at the helm. That ensured its later downfall, after which its hall, chapel and other buildings were taken over by nearby Christ Church.

Durham College, founded by Durham Abbey in the late 13th century for the education of its monks, received a large endowment from the bishop of Durham in 1381, after which it increased its intake to eight student monks and eight seculars – four from north Yorkshire and four from the diocese of Durham.

This large cash injection also financed the laying out of a quadrangle, surrounded by a chapel, library, refectory and living quarters. After the college was surrendered to the Crown it was left vacant for several years, but some of its buildings survive as part of Durham Quad at Trinity College, founded by the self-made politician Thomas Pope.

Oxford roll~call 2

Magdalen
Cardinal Thomas Wolsey, William Camden, Oscar Wilde, T. E. Lawrence, John Paul Getty, John Betjeman, Wilfred Thesiger, Dudley Moore, Norman Davies, James Fenton, Ian Hislop, William Hague, George Osborne

Mansfield
Adam von Trott (see page 123)

Merton
William of Ockham, Lord Randolph Churchill, Max Beerbohm, T. S. Eliot, Keith Douglas, Edward Lucie-Smith, Kris Kristofferson, Howard Davies

New
Sydney Smith, William Spooner, John Galsworthy, A. P. Herbert, Duff Cooper, Maurice Bowra, John Sparrow, Hugh Gaitskell, Tony Benn, John Julius Norwich, John Fowles, Dennis Potter

Oriel
Walter Raleigh, Gilbert White, Beau Brummell, Cecil Rhodes, A. J. P. Taylor

Pembroke
Thomas Browne, Dr Samuel Johnson, George Whitefield, William Blackstone, James Smithson, John Snagge, Michael Heseltine

Queen's (full title **The Queen's College**)
King Henry V, Thomas Middleton, Edmond Halley, Joseph Addison, Jeremy Bentham, Walter Pater, Ernest Dowson, Leopold Stokowski, Edmund Blunden, Oliver Sacks, Tim Berners-Lee

St Anne's
U. A. Fanthorpe, Sister Wendy Beckett, Penelope Lively, Jill Paton Walsh, Jenny Uglow, Susan Sontag, Polly Toynbee, Libby Purves, Edwina Currie, Simon Rattle

St Catherine's
Michael Billington, Joseph Heller, Richard Mabey, John Birt, Peter Mandelson, Jeanette Winterson, Matthew Pinsent

St Edmund Hall (a.k.a. **Teddy Hall**)
Robin Day, John Wells, Gabriel Josipovici, Kevin Crossley-Holland, Terry Jones, Keir Starmer, Samira Ahmed

St Hilda's
Barbara Pym, Kate Millett, Marilyn Butler, Hermione Lee, Wendy Cope, Susan Greenfield

St Hugh's
Mary Renault, Barbara Castle, Joanna Trollope, Liz Forgan, Theresa May, Ruth Lawrence

St John's
Edmund Campion, William Laud, Jethro Tull, A. E. Housman, Robert Graves, Kingsley Amis, Philip Larkin, Simon Jenkins, David Cannadine

Pressing matters

The university first became involved in the print trade as early as the 1480s, but what set it on course to become the largest university press in the world was the 'Great Charter' of 1636 negotiated by the chancellor, William Laud, and granted by Charles I. Laud, who doubled up as the archbishop of Canterbury, foresaw a press of international standing operated on university premises, with its own staff and editorial control – and overseen by an official known as the Architypographus.

The new enterprise was empowered to compete with the Stationers' Company, with which it would quarrel on and off for more than 50 years. One valuable privilege that Laud extracted from the Crown was the printing of the Authorised or King James Version of the Bible, and editions of the Scriptures would bring in large sums for centuries to come.

Today, Oxford University Press (OUP) employs 4,000 people, publishes 6,000 titles worldwide each year and contributes at least £12 million annually to the university kitty.

Unfortunately the Civil War was to bring a temporary check to the Press and a permanent one to the archbishop, whose High Church leanings angered the Puritans. Accused of treason by the Long Parliament of 1640, he was eventually tried in the spring of 1644, and although no convincing evidence was brought against him – and Charles issued an ineffectual pardon – he was beheaded the following January.

With the Restoration in 1660, John Fell (vice-chancellor, dean of Christ Church, bishop of Oxford) took up the baton, and Laud's vision began to become a reality.

felled in verse

A stanza about John Fell is said to have been written by the satirical poet Tom Brown who, accused of a misdemeanour when a scholar at Christ Church, was offered forgiveness if he could translate an epigram by Martial off the top of his head. He enjoyed himself:

> I do not like thee, Doctor Fell,
> The reason why I cannot tell;
> But this I know, and know full well,
> I do not like thee, Doctor Fell.

Fell installed printing presses in the cellars of the newly built Sheldonian Theatre, introducing a large stock of typographical punches and matrices ('Fell Types') from the Dutch Republic, and employing two Dutch typefounders for good measure.

Alongside a range of academic and religious publications, he launched the *Oxford Almanack*, an illustrated calendar which, remarkably, has appeared every year since 1674.

The Oxford comma

Welcome to Pedants' Corner, and a word about the Oxford, or serial, or Harvard comma. You may never have heard of it, but you've just seen one – after the word 'serial'. Many publishers do away with commas at the end of a list and before a conjunction, but OUP remains true to its orthographical tradition.

This book is generally happy without it, but there are times when its absence creates a regrettable confusion, as in this praise of a versatile academic: 'He wrote memorable essays about the metaphysical poets, Margaret Thatcher and Mick Jagger.'

In 1713 Nicholas Hawskmoor designed a new home for the OUP, the Clarendon Building, next door to the Sheldonian. It would remain there until 1830, when a burst of expansion led it to its present headquarters on the corner of Walton Street and Great Clarendon Street, northwest of the centre.

The great project of the Victorian era was an ambitious work first offered to the Press in 1879 by editor James Murray and the Philological Society as *A New English Dictionary on Historical Principles* – eventually to emerge as the *Oxford English Dictionary*. Optimistic estimates reckoned that the work would take ten years to complete for an outlay of £9,000. The reality was that the first edition began to appear in print in 1884 and that it wasn't completed until 1928 – by which time it had cost around £375,000.

This financial burden demanded a fresh initiative, and under its Publisher to the University, Henry Frowde, OUP now moved into popular literature – acquiring the World's Classics and dipping its toe in the waters of medicine and children's literature.

Brothers in Christ

They lived in more gentle times than the Lollards, but the Methodists – who also sprang from Oxford – likewise adopted a name given to them as an insult: it was meant to suggest a pious priggishness.

The movement was launched by the brothers John and Charles Wesley, the elder a don at Lincoln, the younger an undergraduate at Christ Church. In 1729 they formed the Holy Club, its members earnestly drawing on the Bible to examine their spiritual lives, taking food to the poor, visiting prisoners and teaching orphans to read.

John was an indefatigable preacher (he once sermonised for a full two hours at St Mary's), while Charles penned thousands of hymns. Their fellow enthusiast George Whitefield was a servitor at Pembroke (a poor student who, in return for tuition, was obliged to act as a menial servant for well-heeled undergraduates). He was so ardent for the faith that he would pray alone in Christ Church Meadow for hours at a stretch – literally, as he'd perform his devotions lying face down on the grass.

There's a plaque on the building in New Inn Hall Street where John Wesley gave his first sermons (effectively the earliest Methodist meeting house), but the brothers' Methodism failed to catch fire in Oxford itself.

They left Oxford for America in 1735. Nonconformists wouldn't be admitted to the university for well over 100 years – by which time Methodism was firmly rooted not only in the industrial cities of Britain but in areas of British influence all around the world.

Some hymns by Oxford men

Charles Wesley (Methodist, Christ Church)

Hark! the Herald Angels Sing
Jesu, Lover of My Soul
Love Divine, All Loves Excelling
O, For a Thousand Tongues to Sing

John Henry Newman (Roman Catholic, Trinity)

Lead, Kindly Light
Praise to the Holiest in the Height

Reginald Heber (Anglican, Brasenose)

From Greenland's Icy Mountains
Brightest and Best

Henry Milman (Anglican, Brasenose)

Ride on, Ride on in Majesty

Oxford roll-call 3

St Peter's
Revd W. Awdry, Ken Loach, Paul Condon, Matt Frei, Hugh Fearnley-Whittingstall

Somerville
Rose Macaulay, Vera Brittain, Dorothy L. Sayers, Penelope Fitzgerald, Indira Gandhi, Iris Murdoch, A. S. Byatt, Shirley Williams, Esther Rantzen, Emma Kirkby

Trinity
Henry Ireton, Walter Savage Landor, John Henry Newman, Richard Burton (explorer and translator), William Palgrave, Arthur Quiller-Couch, Laurence Binyon, George Butterworth, Terence Rattigan, Anthony Crosland

University
John Radcliffe, Percy Bysshe Shelley, C. S. Lewis, V. S. Naipaul, Lord Robert Cecil, Richard Ingrams, Stephen Hawking, Bill Clinton, Andrew Motion, Max Hastings

Wadham
Christopher Wren, Francis Kilvert, C. B. Fry, Thomas Beecham, Cecil Day Lewis, Alan Bullock, Michael Foot, Melvyn Bragg, Rt Revd Rowan Williams, Monica Ali, Marcus du Sautoy

Worcester
Thomas de Quincey, J. B. Morton, Roger Hollis, Rupert Murdoch, Richard Adams, Woodrow Wyatt, Jeremy Greenstock

Time for a shake-up

During the early Victorian period the university was as much in need of change as its publishing arm, and a royal commission appointed in 1850 issued a damning verdict. The age of the poor scholar was long gone.

- The colleges were much richer – and therefore more powerful – than the university itself.

- The fellows (nearly 550 of them) operated a virtual closed shop. Only 22 posts were open to competition, the rest restricted to candidates from particular districts, schools or families. Of 113 fellows elected to All Souls between 1814 and 1857, 78 were related to the founder.

- All the fellows were unmarried and in holy orders. They held office for life, and many of them lived away from Oxford.

The effect on the quality of education was obvious. One national paper claimed that the only questions put to prospective students were about 'their genealogy and their tailor'. In a Commons debate, one MP urged that 'the healthy fresh breeze of the nineteenth century play through her sequestered cloisters'.

The required religious affiliation of fellows and students (dissenters, let alone atheists, were barred) was tackled by reformers in acts of parliament over the following years.

- The Oxford University Act 1854 ended religious tests for matriculation or bachelors' degrees.
- Gladstone's Universities Tests Act 1871 removed such tests for any office or teaching position, and for any degree except Divinity.
- The Universities of Oxford and Cambridge Act 1877 removed the restriction of college fellowships to clergymen, except for college chaplains and professors of divinity. Dons at last could marry!

Smells and bells

While the university became increasingly secular, a group of Oxford men campaigned for Anglicanism to embrace the rituals of its Roman Catholic heritage. The so-called Oxford (or Tractarian) Movement led to Anglo-Catholicism with its vestments, confessionals and incense (what critics called 'smells and bells'), and its increasing influence was won at the expense of both ridicule and violence.

Several of the movement's founders were Fellows of Oriel: John Keble (whose phenomenally successful *The Christian Year* brought an appointment to the Chair of Poetry), Edward Pusey, Richard Froude and, most famously of all, John Henry Newman – who began his religious life as a Calvinist, but travelled so far in the other direction as to convert to Roman Catholicism.

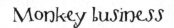

Monkey business

In June 1860, seven months after the publication of Charles Darwin's *On the Origin of Species*, more than 1,000 people crammed into the new Oxford University Museum of Natural History on Parks Road to hear a vigorous debate on evolution.

No transcript survives, but the most eloquent opponent of the theory, the bishop of Oxford, Samuel Wilberforce, is supposed to have asked the biologist Thomas Huxley whether he was happy to have a monkey as an ancestor. Huxley's reported response was that he would be happier to share kinship with a primate than with a man who used his great talents to deny the truth. Darwin himself, unfortunately, was too ill to attend.

Not so obedient

The founders of Keble College, which was named in honour of the great Tractarian John Keble and opened its doors to its first students in 1870, envisaged a High Church atmosphere, with scholars dedicated to 'poverty and obedience'.

Tractarian sympathisers were tapped for funds – among them William Gibbs, the benefactor of the chapel, whose family wealth derived from Peruvian guano (bird droppings, used as fertiliser and as an ingredient in explosives).

The founders' ideals proved difficult to enforce. The first warden, Edward Talbot, not only taught science but sympathised with the theory of evolution, and at popular, unlicensed boxing matches 'the liquid refreshment was not tea'.

William Butterfield designed the buildings in the polychromatic brick which had become a trademark of High Church architecture, though its detractors termed it the 'holy zebra' style. A surely apocryphal story has a French visitor echoing General Bosquet's comment that the Charge of the Light Brigade wasn't war as he recognised it: 'C'est magnifique, mais ce n'est pas la gare?' ('It's magnificent, but isn't it the station?')

This ardent group – often known as the Tractarians because of the more than 90 tracts they issued between 1833 and 1841 – tried to scupper the appointment of a one-time Oriel man, Renn Hampden, as Regius Professor of Divinity in 1836 because of his liberal views. On this occasion, however, their zeal was ineffective.

Here come the girls

In *A Room of One's Own*, published in 1928, Virginia Woolf writes of straying onto the lawn of an unnamed Oxbridge college and finding herself accosted by 'a curious-looking object, in a cut-away coat and evening shirt':

> His face expressed horror and indignation. Instinct rather than reason came to my help; he was a Beadle; I was a woman. This was the turf; there was the path. Only the Fellows and Scholars are allowed here; the gravel is the place for me.

Women had been allowed into Oxford for some years – but grudgingly, and until very recently on inferior terms to the men.

In 1875 a new statute allowed the university to create examinations for women, and soon four women's colleges were up and running: Lady Margaret Hall, 1878; Somerville College, 1879; St Hugh's, 1886; and St Hilda's, 1893. (St Anne's would follow much later, in 1952.)

It wasn't until 1920, though, that women were accepted as full members of the university and allowed to take degrees.

A second chance

Ruskin College (an affiliate of the university) was established in 1899 by two American Oxford graduates to provide an education for men whose academic background was too meagre to allow them to enrol as regular undergraduates. Today, of course, it accepts women, too.

The college's mission is to change the lives of working people by giving them a 'second chance' of a first-rate education. Closely linked to the labour movement, it has a curriculum geared to the social sciences – and many of its graduates have gone on to make an impact in the world of politics and public affairs.

'But a girl of seventeen is not always thinking of books, especially in the Oxford summer term.'

Mary A. Ward

In 1927 a quota was imposed, ruling that no more than 25 per cent of undergraduates could be women (this wasn't abolished until 1957), and only in 1959 were the women's colleges awarded full collegiate status.

As for the dons, Agnes Headlam-Morley (St Hugh's) was the first woman to be appointed to a full professorship, when she became Montague Burton Professor of Industrial Relations in October 1948, while in 1973 Balliol was the first of the traditional all-male colleges to elect a woman as a fellow and tutor (Carol Clark, who taught French).

The male–female divide was breached in 1974 when five men's colleges (Brasenose, Jesus, Hertford, St Catherine's and Wadham) opened their doors to women students. The others followed suit, the last to fall in line being Oriel, ten years later.

As for the women-only colleges, Lady Margaret Hall and St Anne's first admitted men in 1979, St Hugh's in 1986 and Somerville in 1994 – leaving St Hilda's to hold out in glorious isolation until October 2008.

Britain's first woman premier, Margaret Thatcher (Somerville), was given a gigantic snub in 1985 when – on a vote of 738 to 319 – the university refused her the honorary degree given to every other prime minister since the war. It was a protest against her cuts in education spending

Rhodes scholars

The will of the English-born South African businessman and politician Cecil Rhodes provided for the prestigious Rhodes Scholarships, which since 1902 have brought high-flying overseas students to study at Oxford.

Notable Rhodes scholars include the former US poet laureate Robert Penn Warren, the singer and actor Kris Kristofferson, the feminist writer Naomi Woolf, and the former US president Bill Clinton.

Today's university can claim to be in tune with the times, not only in its equal ratio of men to women but in striving to find more places for students from unprivileged backgrounds. The federal nature of its structure, though, is apt to confuse the outsider.

• The **university** sets the exams, and its academic departments provide facilities for teaching and research, determine the syllabuses, and deliver lectures and seminars. The lecturers are scattered around the colleges, where they also teach. Individual faculties (English, Philosophy, Music and so on) have their own libraries.

• The autonomous **colleges** arrange tutorials for their undergraduates and look after their general wellbeing, housing many of them in college buildings. Each college has its own library, too.

It follows that some of the venerable buildings you see around the centre of Oxford are college buildings, while others belong to the university. It's time we had a look at some of them...

Oxford at No. 10

Twenty-seven British prime ministers have been educated at the university. They are listed here with their dates of office.

Earl of Wilmington 1742–1743 (Trinity)
Henry Pelham 1743–1754 (Hart Hall)
George Grenville 1763–1765 (Christ Church)
Earl of Chatham 1766–1768 (Trinity)
Lord North 1770–1782 (Trinity)
Earl of Shelburne 1782–1783
  (Christ Church)
Duke of Portland 1783, 1807–1809
  (Christ Church)
Henry Addington 1801–1804 (Brasenose)
Lord Grenville 1806–1807 (Christ Church)
Earl of Liverpool 1812–1817
  (Christ Church)
George Canning 1827 (Christ Church)
Sir Robert Peel 1841–1846 (Christ Church)
Earl of Derby 1852, 1858–1859, 1866–1868
  (Christ Church)
William Ewart Gladstone 1868–1874, 1880–
  1885, 1886, 1892–1894 (Christ Church)

Marquess of Salisbury 1885–1886, 1886–1892, 1895–1902 (Christ Church)

Earl of Rosebery 1894–1895 (Christ Church)

Herbert Asquith 1908–1916 (Balliol)

Clement Attlee 1945–1951 (University)

Anthony Eden 1955–1957 (Christ Church)

Harold Macmillan 1957–1963 (Balliol)

Sir Alec Douglas-Home 1963–1964 (Christ Church)

Harold Wilson 1964–1970, 1974–1976 (Jesus)

Edward Heath 1970–1974 (Balliol)

Margaret Thatcher 1979–1990 (Somerville)

Tony Blair 1997–2007 (St John's)

David Cameron 2010–2016 (Brasenose)

Theresa May 2016-Present (St Hugh's College)

'To call a man an Oxford man is to pay him the highest compliment that can be paid to a human being.'

Oriel Square

The tower of St Mary the Virgin dominates
this view of Oriel Square, which lies to the
south of the High Street, just outside the area
described in this chapter. Oriel College is on
the right. Note the projecting window, known
as an oriel window, above the front door; it
seems that the college took its name from a
similar window on its original building.

CHAPTER four

BEHIND THE WALLS

A brief tour of central Oxford

It's time to explore the dense cluster of ancient buildings between Broad Street to the north and High Street to the south. Our eastern boundary will be Catte Street, we'll return to the Broad along Turl Street, and along the way we'll pass no fewer than eight colleges, a celebrated bookshop, the university church and one of the world's greatest libraries.

Bicycles are Oxford's favourite form of transport (most of these streets are wholly or partly closed to motor vehicles), but let's set off on foot so that we have time to stand and stare.

Broad Street

We begin our walking tour at the western end of the Broad, facing **Balliol College**. Note the cross inlaid in the road which marks the spot where the three Protestant martyrs (see pages 43–44) were burned to death. Inside the college, under an archway between two quads, is a gate blackened by scorch marks, the damage supposedly caused by the flames that engulfed Thomas Cranmer in 1556. If so, the pyre was surely rather too close to the building for comfort.

Since the college has the reputation of being more worldly than most (it has, for example, produced three prime ministers), it's fitting that it was allegedly founded, around 1263, because of a drunken indiscretion. The wealthy John Balliol of Barnard Castle in County Durham was apparently abusive towards the bishop of Durham while in his cups, and was obliged to put up the money for a new foundation as an act of penance.

Visit **Trinity College**, next door, on a day when it's open to the public and you'll gawp at the evidence of traditional privilege. As we've seen (page 99), it replaced the suppressed Durham College in 1555. With some 400 students (300 of them undergraduates), it's not the largest in terms of numbers, but it stands in extensive grounds – and its estimated endowment funds in 2010 stood at more than £80 million. It's not the richest, though.

A Hitler victim

The lawyer and diplomat Adam von Trott (1909–1944) is one of five Germans commemorated on Balliol's Second World War memorial, and he's also recorded among the war dead in the Rotunda at Rhodes House.

Von Trott, who before the war had attempted to raise international support for internal resistance against the Nazis – he lobbied the British government and unavailingly visited the United States – was hanged in Berlin's Plötzensee prison on 26 August 1944.

In our roll-call (page 100), we've included him under Mansfield, where he was a Rhodes scholar. The college wasn't formally part of the university until 1955, however, so students had to matriculate through other colleges – in his case, Balliol.

Trinity and Balliol have long had a less than neighbourly rivalry, with taunting songs known as 'Gordouli' chanted over the dividing garden wall. In Dorothy L. Sayers' novel *Five Red Herrings*, Lord Peter Wimsey, a Balliol man, denies having known any of his contemporaries from Trinity: 'The Jews have no dealings with the Samaritans,' he says.

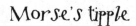

Morse's tipple

Sandwiched between two departments of Blackwell's bookshop in the Broad is the **White Horse**, a favourite haunt of Colin Dexter's Inspector Morse. If you'd like to follow in the inspector's bibulous footsteps, here are a few more Oxford watering holes he favours:

The Eagle and Child in St Giles (owned by neighbouring St John's College). Dexter himself enjoyed a pint here, as did C. S. Lewis and J. R. R. Tolkien in days gone by.

The Bear in Alfred Street – the oldest and one of the smallest pubs in Oxford.

The Turf Tavern, off Holywell (see page 39).

The Randolph Hotel in Beaumont Street. It even has a Morse Bar.

On the south side of the Broad we see the **Museum of the History of Science** in the Old Ashmolean building, but we'll keep resolutely to the north side in search of that bookworm's delight, **Blackwell's bookshop**.

Benjamin Blackwell, son of the city's first librarian, founded the shop in 1879 (though it then occupied a very small part of its present space), and within 20 years he had begun a publishing arm, too. On his death in 1924 his son Basil took over the business, and 'the gaffer', as he was known, was still pottering about his Oxford empire well into the 1980s.

While the publishing business was sold in 2007, the bookselling has expanded to 60 outlets nationwide. The original premises contains the gem of all Aladdin-like browsing experiences. The vast Norrington Room – opened in 1966 and named after Sir Arthur Norrington, a former president of Trinity College – extends under part of Trinity, has 3 miles (5 km) of shelving and, at 10,000 square feet (930 square metres) is credited by the *Guinness Book of Records* as being the world's largest single room selling books.

Ten books set in Oxford

Jude the Obscure In which our poor, self-taught, working-class hero Jude Fawley tragically fails to infiltrate the academic fastnesses of Thomas Hardy's Oxford look-alike, Christminster.

Zuleika Dobson Max Beerbohm's crazy satire of 1911 on the sheltered collegiate world. Its heroine, granddaughter of the warden of Judas College (based on the author's Merton), is so madly attractive that every last Oxford undergraduate commits suicide for love of her.

Brideshead Revisited Evelyn Waugh's hero Charles Ryder (a student at humble Hertford, as was Waugh) meets the gilded and seductive Lord Sebastian Flyte (Christ Church, naturally), and is introduced to a world of high living and Roman Catholicism.

Tom Brown at Oxford Thomas Hughes (Oriel) is best known for *Tom Brown's Schooldays*, but this is the sequel of 1861.

Gaudy Night Dorothy L. Sayers was one of the first women to get an Oxford degree, and her thriller is a tale of intrigue at her alma mater Somerville, thinly disguised as Shrewsbury College. At one level it's an exploration of women's right to a first-rate education.

The Gaudy The first book in the *Staircase in Surrey* quintet by J. I. M. Stewart (Oriel), Oxford don, literary critic and the author of dozens of crime novels and short stories under the pseudonym Michael Innes.

An Instance of the Fingerpost An epistolary novel of 1997 by Iain Pears (Wadham), involving four unreliable narrators and set in the city in 1663 – soon after the Restoration of the Monarchy, with the authority of Charles II not yet settled and conspiracies rife.

Jill Wartime novel by Philip Larkin (St John's), in which a gauche northern grammar-school boy comes up to Oxford and meets dissipated southerners.

Last Bus to Woodstock The first of the 13 Inspector Morse books by Colin Dexter (Christ's College, Cambridge, alas), all of which are based in the city.

Lyra's Oxford Philip Pullman (Exeter) set his Dark Materials trilogy here, but this story gets our vote not only for actually naming the place in its title, but for even including a map of Lyra's alternative Oxford, along with adverts and tourist information.

The fortress-like building east of Blackwell's (designed by Sir Giles Gilbert Scott) reminds us of the huge inflow of funds to Oxford from wealthy individuals and international companies. This is the **New Bodleian**, built as an overspill depository for the Bodleian Library itself, and two-thirds of its cost was met by the Rockefeller Foundation. (Wealth, alas, doesn't ensure perfection. When George VI officially opened the building in 1940, the ceremonial silver key broke in the lock.)

In 2015, after a major revamp paid for by the Garfield Weston Foundation, it became the **Weston Library**, housing the Bodleian's special collections of rare manuscripts, books and maps, and with new research facilities and exhibition galleries. Learning is expensive.

But beneficence on such a scale isn't anything new. Sir Christopher Wren's **Sheldonian Theatre**, across the street, is named after Gilbert Sheldon, who was not only the chancellor of the university at the time but, most important of all, the building's chief financial backer.

Apart from staging degree ceremonies, the

building is used for lectures, conferences and concerts: Handel conducted the first performance of his oratorio *Athalia* here in 1733. An eight-sided cupola floods the interior with light (you can walk up inside it for views across Oxford), while the oil-on-canvas ceiling paintings, restored in 2008, are the work of Robert Streater, court painter to Charles II. They show Truth conferring her blessing on the Arts and Sciences and – as if it were needed – expelling ignorance from the university.

And whose are those heads on the 13 plinths outside? They were last restored in the 1970s by the sculptor Michael Black, who also replaced the four on the Science Museum next door, but nobody knows who the originals were supposed to be. In his novel *Zuleika Dobson*, Max Beerbohm refers to them as 'emperors', and that idea has stuck. 'Who were lechers,' he wrote, 'they are without bodies; who were tyrants, they are crowned never but with crowns of snow; who made themselves even with the gods, they are by American visitors frequently mistaken for the Twelve Apostles.'

Next door to the Sheldonian is a Palladian frontage designed by Wren's greatest pupil. The **Clarendon Building**, as we've seen (page 105), was built to house the Oxford University Press. It was financed largely from the proceeds of the highly profitable *History of the Great Rebellion* by Edward Hyde, 1st Earl of Clarendon, whose trust fund also paid for the building of the Clarendon Laboratory in Parks Road.

Catte Street

Facing us at the crossroads is the former **Indian Institute**, built in 1883 to provide training for the Indian civil service. We turn right into Catte Street (formerly just plain Cat Street) and almost immediately come across that favourite of guide books and calendars, the **Bridge of Sighs**, which spans New College Lane to link the Old and New Quads of **Hertford College** (see pages 94–95).

The university has always enjoyed its spats, and the bridge almost inevitably became a *cause célèbre*. As soon as the college was given permission to build a new quad in 1899, its principal suggested that there should be a tunnel under the road for servants and provisions, and a bridge for fellows and undergraduates. The warden and fellows of New College immediately complained that they would lose the view of their chapel and tower. There was town as well as rival gown opposition, too, and the controversy dragged on for years.

In the event, the tunnel idea was dropped and – New College having at last relented – in February 1913 the city council agreed that Hertford could have its bridge.

Skywatching

The remarkable scientist Edmond Halley (1656–1742), who correctly computed the orbit of the comet which bears his name, installed an observatory in his house at no. 7 New College Lane, and there's a plaque on the wall to commemorate the fact.

Halley came down from Queen's College without taking his degree, but later became not only Savilian Professor of Geometry at the university but also the country's second Astronomer Royal.

The architect was Sir Thomas Jackson, who had designed much of Hertford's two quads, had been busy at Brasenose and Trinity, and would clad his Bridge of Sighs with the same white Clipsham stone he had used for the Examination Schools in the High.

A college guide describes it as 'so much more beautiful than its distant inspiration in Venice'. Jackson himself admitted that its strangeness in such a setting invited criticism, adding, 'I have tried to give the design a character rather in conformity with the traditions of the English Renaissance.'

Crossing the road from Hertford's gatehouse we arrive at the academic centrepiece of our tour, the **Bodleian Library**. It was founded in 1602 by Thomas Bodley (see page 46), who made an agreement with the Stationers' Company in London to house a copy of every book they registered. Today it's one of six copyright libraries in the UK and Ireland entitled to a copy of every title that comes off the presses, with the result that its vast collection of 11 million printed items is largely stored out of sight – much of it below ground.

A tunnel under the Broad links the old and new libraries, and – until 2010, when a large warehouse near Swindon replaced the New Bodleian as a storage facility – a mechanical conveyor and a pneumatic tube system used to ferry books from one side to the other. Scholars who relish an underground experience can instead do their reading in the Gladstone Link – a tunnel formerly used to take books from the Bodleian to the **Radcliffe Camera** (see page 52) next door, and converted in 2011 into an open-shelf library.

Bodley was sniffy about the books he kept. He had a battered first folio of Shakespeare's plays inherited from the earlier Duke Humfrey's Library, and once he had acquired a much smarter third folio he thought the original inferior – one of what he called 'idle books and riff-raffs' – and he sold it. Much later, in the late 19th century, a man brought a first folio to the Bodleian for identification, and a bright young librarian recognised it as the very copy which had gone missing all those years before. The library had to raise the then very large sum of £3,000 to buy it back. (It would cost about £3 million today.)

133

Gaping mouths

Keep your eyes open as you explore Oxford for the many stone gargoyles and grotesques which adorn the old buildings. The former spout water, whereas the latter are decorations pure (though sometimes decidedly impure) and simple.

Because the stone used is not very durable, most of the figures are not as old as you might expect. The newest of them, unveiled by the writer Philip Pullman in 2009, are to be seen on the northwest wall of the Bodleian. A competition among local schoolchildren produced nine winning designs to replace medieval grotesques which had become weatherworn beyond repair.

Although Pullman spoke of 'a long and proud tradition of rudeness, mischief and disobedience', the nine new carvings are respectable additions to the Bodleian façade. They range from heads of Sir Thomas Bodley and General Pitt Rivers to a dodo, a Green Man and fictional characters with Oxford connections, including C. S. Lewis's Aslan, Lewis Carroll's Tweedledum and Tweedledee, and myths and monsters from J. R. R. Tolkien's fantasy world.

The treasures of the Bodleian are legion. For an exhibition in 2011 the curator asked every member of staff to select a favourite item, and then whittled down by a half the 150 books, maps, letters and documents they regarded as must-see items. Here are just a few of them:

- One of four surviving copies of Magna Carta.
- A pristine copy of the Gutenberg Bible.
- A 14th-century copy of Marco Polo's *Travels*.
- The earliest almost complete copy of a poem by Sappho, rescued from a rubbish dump in Egypt during the 19th century.
- A 13th-century bestiary showing an elephant being strangled by a dragon.
- The Codex Mendoza, an account made for the first Spanish viceroy of the Aztec kingdom.
- Jane Austen's handwritten compendium of her own earliest writings.
- Mary Shelley's draft of *Frankenstein*, with scribbled suggestions by Percy Shelley.

There are several more Shelley artefacts at the Bodleian, including the poet's watch and chain, five seals, and a guitar – an instrument he held but briefly, as he bought it as a present for the musician Jane Williams, with whom he was infatuated.

Behind the Radcliffe Camera, across the cobbles of Radcliffe Square, is **Brasenose College**, founded in 1509 and affectionately known as BNC. In its chapel you'll find a sombre reminder of town-and-gown violence. The memorial to an undergraduate killed by a butcher's knife in 1857 bears the epitaph *Inter tumultum plebis obdormivit*: 'He fell asleep among the tumult of the people.'

Between Brasenose and Lincoln – which we'll visit later – there's a door which is unlocked for five minutes each year, on Ascension Day, to allow the passage of celebrants beating the bounds (see page 174).

To our south is the magnificent pile of St Mary's Church, but although its main entrance is now on Radcliffe Square, we'll save our description of it until we reach the High.

Now we return to Catte Street and, next door to Hertford, a college with a difference, **All Souls**. Its official title is long-winded, although it's not unique in that: The Warden and the College of the Souls of all Faithful People Deceased in the University of Oxford.

Harry Potter in Oxford

If you can't beat 'em, join 'em! Many young visitors want nothing more than to explore locations used in the Harry Potter films, so here's our 'potted' guide:

Divinity School, Bodleian library. It's used for the Hogwarts sanatorium.

Duke Humfrey's Library, also part of the Bodleian. The Hogwarts library (of course).

Christ Church dining hall. Hogwarts dining hall, hammerbeam roof and all, used in the sorting ceremony.

Christ Church cloisters. Used for various scenes: can you spot where Harry is shown the trophy his father won as a seeker in Quidditch?

New College. The scene of several 'Goblet of Fire' quadrangle shots, including the moment when Mad-Eye Moody turns Draco Malfoy into a white ferret.

Pitt Rivers Museum. Some say its interior was the inspiration for Diagon Alley – but you'll have to judge for yourself.

The difference lies in the fact that it's a research institution with no undergraduates. All of its members automatically become fellows – full members of the governing body. Getting in is incredibly difficult. Only those with first-class degrees from Oxford can apply, and candidates compete for what are usually two places a year (though occasionally nobody at all makes the grade) by taking 'the hardest exam in the world':

- Two papers are on subjects of candidates' choice, from a range of academic categories.

- There are two further papers on general subjects, with candidates choosing from three devilishly devised questions for each one.

- Between four and six likely candidates are invited for a 'viva', or oral examination, before supper with around 75 members in college.

The successful 'examination fellows' have no teaching or research requirements; receive an annual stipend of around £15,000; may study anything at Oxford gratis, with room and board; may pursue approved non-academic careers; and are required only to pursue academia on a part-time basis and attend weekend dinners during their first year.

Disgruntled rejects can at least console themselves with the knowledge that several luminaries have failed before them, including Hilaire Belloc, Lord David Cecil, Lord (Alfred) Denning and Hugh Trevor-Roper.

High Street

A left turn at the junction with the High would take us to down to Magdalen College, via Queen's College on the left and University College and the Examination Schools across the road, but we turn right to find ourselves outside the original front of the university church of **St Mary the Virgin**. The decorated gothic tower dates from 1280 (climb 124 steps for excellent views over the cityscape), and the spire, frantic with pinnacles, gargoyles and statues, from around 1320.

> 'Oxford is a glorious place; godlike!
> I have walked round the colleges
> under the full moon, and thought it
> would be heaven to live and die here.'
>
> *Edward Burne-Jones*

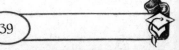

The baroque barley-sugar columns on either side of the ancient porch may first take your eye, but raise your eyes to the Virgin and Child above and ask yourself how the statue came to be so pockmarked: surely the damage is inconsistent with mere weathering?

The answer is that it was the target of fervid Puritans. The statue was designed in 1637 by Nicholas Stone, Charles I's master mason, and was paid for by Dr Morgan Owen, chaplain to the ill-fated Archbishop Laud. The installation of this 'Romish' abomination was one of the charges brought against Laud at his trial (see page 103), and during the Civil War Cromwell's gung-ho troopers took potshots at it. Somehow it survived.

The oldest part of the interior is the chapel added in 1328 by the rector, Adam de Brome – the founder of what became Oriel College, to which he diverted Church revenues and gave special privileges. The chapel functioned as a courtroom in which the chancellor of the university held sway, fixing rents, fining sellers of bad meat and sending miscreants (including a 'scolding woman') to prison.

The humble two-storey building attached to the northeast corner of the church, abutting the tower and opening onto Radcliffe Square, was the very first university (as opposed to college) building in Oxford. It dates from 1320, when the university adopted St Mary's as its administrative centre. The upper room of this congregation house served both as the university's 'bank' – its money was stored in a large chest – and as its first library, with a small collection of chained books. It was in the Old Library in October 1942 that the charity which became Oxfam was founded, its initial campaign the relief of famine in Greece caused by Allied naval blockades during the Second World War.

St Mary's has been a veritable theatre of real-life drama over the centuries. It was here that the Oxford Martyrs were tried (and Cranmer withdrew his recantations of Protestant belief); that Wesley delivered his ringing denunciation of the university's religious apathy ('I am cleared of the blood of these men'); and that Newman (the vicar from 1828) and Keble launched the Oxford, or Tractarian, Movement.

Nobel laureates
who studied at Oxford

(Excluding prize winners who were on the
university staff but didn't matriculate here.
The date given is the date of the award.)

Peace
Viscount Cecil of Chelwood (University, 1937)
Lester B. Pearson (St John's, 1957)
Aung San Suu Kyi (St Hugh's, 1991)
Malala Yousafzai (Lady Magret Hall, 2014)

Medicine
Lord (Howard) Florey (Magdalen, 1945)
Sir Peter Medawar (Magdalen, 1960)
Sir John Eccles (Magdalen, 1963)
Baruch S. Blumberg (Balliol, 1976)
Sir John Vane (St Catherine's, 1982)
Sydney Brenner (Exeter, 2002)
Oliver Smithies (Balliol, 2007)
Sir John Gurdon (Christ Church, 2012)

Literature
John Galsworthy (New, 1932)
T. S. Eliot (Merton, 1948)
William Golding (Brasenose, 1983)
V. S. Naipaul (University, 2001)

Economics
Sir John Hicks (Balliol, 1972)
James E. Meade (Oriel, 1977)
Lawrence Klein (Lincoln, 1980)
A. Michael Spence (Magdalen, 2001)

Chemistry
Frederick Soddy (Merton, 1921)
Sir Cyril Hinshelwood (Balliol, 1956)
Sir Alexander Todd (Oriel, 1957)
Dorothy Hodgkin (Somerville, 1964)
Sir John Cornforth (St Catherine's, 1975)
Sir John Walker (St Catherine's, 1997)

Physics
Sir Martin Ryle (Christ Church, 1974)
Anthony J. Leggett (Balliol, Merton, Magdalen, 2003)
J. Michael Kosterlitz (Brasenose, 2016)

'The clever men of Oxford
Know all that there is to be knowed.
But they none of them know
one half as much
As intelligent Mr Toad.'

Kenneth Grahame, The Wind in the Willows

St Mary's was the venue for graduation and other ceremonies until the building of the Sheldonian Theatre, and it continues to be the focus of the university's spiritual life.

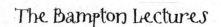

The Bampton Lectures

The will of John Bampton, canon of Salisbury (died 1751), left money for an annual set of lectures to be delivered in St Mary's Church – and, remarkably, they have remained a fixture of the Oxford calendar from 1780 until the present day.

During the great debates of the 19th century they were sometimes controversial. In 1832, for instance, the liberal Renn Hampden (see page 113) enraged the Tractarians, who accused him of Arianism, a heresy which demoted Christ's role in the Trinity.

The rules have been tweaked a little over the years. Bampton stipulated that there should be eight lectures each year 'to confirm and establish the Christian faith, and to confute all heretics and schismatics'. Today they are usually biennial, and heretics are generally spared, but they continue to concentrate on Christian themes – and, for good measure, they're usually published in book form afterwards.

A little further up the road, on the corner with Turl Street, we meet the Grade I listed **All Saints' Church**. Although it was declared redundant in 1971 and became the library of Lincoln College four years later, it has a proud history as the city church (and its full peal of eight bells is still rung by the Oxford Society of Change Ringers), so we'll give it its ecclesiastical, rather than academic, due here.

The original church was founded in 1122, but in March 1700 the spire collapsed, and most of the building was destroyed with it. Twenty years later, after Queen Anne and many of the Oxford colleges rallied round financially, a new church, classical in style, rose from the rubble. Its promotion to city church, where the mayor and corporation worshipped, came in 1896, when St Martin's at Carfax was demolished; St Michael at the North Gate holds this distinction today.

You can still walk among the gravestones outside, while the only major change to the interior during its conversion into a library was the raising of the floor a few feet in order to provide space for the lower reading rooms.

Turl Street

Resisting the temptation to press on towards the covered market and Carfax, we turn right down the Turl to pass three more colleges on our way back to the Broad.

The first, on our right, is **Lincoln**, founded by Richard Fleming in 1427 and afflicted, like All Souls, with a largely unused and cumbersome official title: The College of the Blessed Mary and All Saints. The religious attribution reflected more than simple piety. Fleming, then bishop of Lincoln, intended his new foundation to be a bulwark against the teaching of John Wycliffe's Lollards (see pages 92–93), and he envisaged 'a little college of true students of theology who would defend the mysteries of Scripture against those ignorant laymen who profaned with swinish snouts its most holy pearls'.

The bishop would doubtless have had even stronger things to say had he witnessed the election of John Wesley as a fellow 300 years later. Today, of course, Lincoln is proud of its Methodist connection. The study in which he's believed to have worked is kept as the Wesley Room (American Methodists paid for its renovation early in the 20th century), there's a portrait of him in the hall, and his bust looks down on you from the front quad.

A moral crusade

The American Lutheran pastor Frank Buchman (1878–1961) founded a religious movement which first flickered in Oxford and then flared across the world. He came to the city in 1921, his high-minded evangelism being so popular that his lunchtime meetings, attracting large numbers of dons and undergraduates, could be accommodated only in the ballroom of the Randolph Hotel and, later, the Old Library of St Mary's Church.

The flourishing sect was known as the Oxford Group, but, as its reach extended ever wider, Buchman gave it a new name: Moral Re-Armament. It was, he said, 'a Christian revolution for remaking the world' – and he even attempted to convert Adolf Hitler. In 2001, those Oxford roots long forgotten, it was restyled Initiatives of Change.

The Oxford quads, with their creepered stone buildings grouped around central lawns, are suggestive of the medieval cloisters from which they grew. Lincoln has three of them – Front (15th century), Chapel (1608–1631) and Grove (19th century) – and the cluster has been praised by the architectural guru Nikolaus Pevsner as displaying 'more of the character of a 15th century college than any other in Oxford'.

The former beer cellar below the great hall is among the oldest parts of the college, and is home to the Deep Hall (or 'Deepers') bar.

Open to the public

The glimpse of an ancient quad through an equally ancient doorway is an alluring sight, and the good news is that most of the Oxford colleges are open to the public, although visiting hours are necessarily restricted. (Check online or at the porter's lodge.) Some are free to enter, and most of the others make only a small charge.

The two most expensive offer something extra: Magdalen its riverside walks, Christ Church the cathedral.

Exeter College, next door, is small but is Oxford's fourth oldest. Palmer's Tower in the northeast corner of the front quad dates from 1492, while the vaulted hall (with the college bar beneath) was completed in 1618, and the rest of the quad had taken its present shape by 1710. A few moments in Exeter's history:

- The only authority for Henry VII's date of birth is a 14th-century psalter in the college library. The Tudors used it as a family record, and Katherine of Aragon later wrote in it:

    Thys book ys myn
    Katherine the qwene

- In the Fellows' Garden (with a great view over Radcliffe Square) is a winding path said to have been designed by William Hogarth. Its snaking progress mimics the 'Line of Beauty' which he drew on a palette in his 1745 self-portrait to define his principles of beauty.

- Advising the college on alterations in 1802, the architect John Nash took no fee but asked instead for his portrait to hang in the dining hall – as it still does.

- When a new chapel was designed in 1856 by George Gilbert Scott on the lines of the Sainte-Chapelle in Paris, its 17th-century forerunner proved so stout that it had to be dynamited.

Exeter, as its name suggests, traditionally favoured undergraduates from the West Country. **Jesus**, across the road – dating from 1571, and so Oxford's only Elizabethan foundation – was the Welsh college.

It had a rocky start. Hugh Price, the wealthy clergyman (and treasurer of St David's) who had conveyed his properties in Brecon to the college in return for the right to choose future principals, fellows and scholars, was discovered, on his death, to be not quite so wealthy after all: the houses he had gifted were only mortgaged to him rather than owned, and money had to be raised elsewhere.

Although the university reforms of the mid-19th century put paid to any rigid exclusivity, the Welsh connection persists today.

- Some 15 per cent of undergraduates come from Wales.

- Meyricke Scholarships are available to graduate students in any discipline who hold a first degree from the University of Wales.

- The college is one of the world's centres of excellence for Celtic studies.

Most of the buildings in the Front and Second quads are 17th-century, albeit with some later additions and alterations, while the principal – oh, lucky man! – lives in the lodgings, built at his own expense by the wonderfully named Sir Eubule Thelwall, who ran the college from 1621 until 1630. This building includes, to quote the antiquarian Anthony Wood, 'a very fair dining-room adorned with wainscot curiously engraven'.

As we return the few paces to the Broad, we may perhaps echo the words of Oscar Wilde. After getting off his chest what he disliked about the city, he added an unabashed encomium: 'Oxford still remains the most beautiful thing in England, and nowhere else are life and art so exquisitely blended, so perfectly made one.'

The open spaces of Oxford

Within easy reach of the cloister-like confines of its ancient walls, the city offers several opportunities for visitors to stretch their legs. Here are five of them.

The University Parks

In these 70 acres (28 hectares) on the banks of the Cherwell you'll find some exotic trees; the cricket pavilion designed in 1881 by Sir Thomas Jackson (the ground itself is said to be the only one in the UK where you can watch first-class cricket for free); a 'genetic garden' (it demonstrates evolutionary processes); and High Bridge (more usually known as the Rainbow Bridge), erected in 1923–1924 to give work to the unemployed.

A bench near the riverbank carries the puzzling inscription ORE STABIT FORTIS ARARE PLACET ORE STAT. Any ideas?*

Magdalen College Deer Park

Otherwise known as The Grove, this was thickly wooded until the onset of Dutch elm disease in the 1970s. Addison's Walk takes you to The Meadow on the banks of the Cherwell, a riot of the delicate snake's head fritillary in the spring.

---

*It looks like Latin, but makes no sense – a literal translation would be: 'By mouth it will stand strong to plough it pleases by mouth it stands.' But rearrange the spaces between the words, and you'll find that it's everyday English.

The Botanic Garden

Across the road from Magdalen, this is one of the oldest scientific gardens in the world. It began in 1621 as a physic garden, growing plants for medicinal research. Today there are some 5,000 species on the 5-acre (2-hectare) site, making it, as the website proudly claims, 'one of the most biodiverse areas of land in the world'. Entry is free to children, and to students and staff of Oxford's two universities.

Christ Church Meadow

You don't have to pass through the college lodge to reach this tranquil spot, which has the Isis flowing along one side and the Cherwell on the other. A herd of Longhorn cattle complements the Magdalen deer. The gates open early to give access to the boathouses: this is where university rowing events take place.

Port Meadow

A little further out, to the northwest, these 440 acres (178 hectares) form the largest area of common land in Oxford. Prehistoric people were here (see page 20), but the soil has never been ploughed or farmed. Large areas are flooded for much of the year, attracting flocks of migratory birds. A popular walk of less than an hour takes you from the Trout Inn at Wolvercote to the other end of the meadow at the Perch, Binsey.

University challenge

Oxford rowers train for the Boat Race during floods on the Isis in 1872.

CHAPTER five

VICTORIAN AND MODERN OXFORD

We paused our pell-mell history of the city during a terrible outbreak of cholera in 1832, awaiting the typical brisk Victorian response to public squalor. In fact there were further epidemics in 1849 and 1854, and although the Thames Conservancy declared that noxious discharges into the river must end by 1868, the authorities didn't get started on a new sewerage system for another five years. By 1880 some three-quarters of the houses in Oxford were connected, but New Botley had to wait until 1884 and Summertown until 1890.

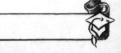

Some 19th-century highlights

1844 The railway comes to Oxford, with the Great Western's line from Didcot. The station is moved to its present site in 1852.

1845 The present Ashmolean Museum in Beaumont Street opens, designed by Charles Cockerell – a descendant of the 17th-century diarist Samuel Pepys.

1860 Oxford University Museum of Natural History opens in Parks Road.

1873 Work begins on a new sewer system, some 33 miles (53 km) of tunnels and drains being laid by 1880.

1884 General Augustus Pitt Rivers donates his archaeological and anthropological collections to the university. By 1886 they are housed in a purpose-built museum adjacent to the Museum of Natural History.

1892 Opening of the city's first electricity generating station.

1893 New town hall built in St Aldate's.

1894 Oliver Lodge gives the world's first public demonstration of wireless telegraphy at the Oxford Museum of Natural History.

Even less fortunate were Headington, Iffley, New Marston and the more distant parts of Cowley: they wouldn't be ushered into the brave new sanitary world until around 1920.

The age of steam

The first Victorian revolution arrived courtesy of the Great Western Railway, which brought its line down from Didcot in 1844. It was soon followed by the London & North Western, which ran two further lines to Bletchley and Banbury. The broad-gauge GWR and the standard-gauge LNWR had their own separate stations, the latter on the site of the long-gone Rewley Abbey.

Almost overnight, a world of coaching inns and livery stables disappeared. A survey of Oxford inns by Samuel Griffiths, who owned both the Angel and the Star and employed more than 90 people, revealed that during 1834–1835 more than 13,000 travellers stayed in the city, however briefly. Most came by stagecoach – many of the horses provided by Charles Symonds, who kept more than 100 in his livery stable at 30 Holywell Street.

For some towns the railway brought a new prosperity, boosting exports or luring tourists, but Oxford – with no serious industry and limited attractions – could only look on as the trains steamed through on their way to other destinations. The city had effectively been bypassed, and at a time of national recession that meant local hardship.

Dampened spirits

The antiquarian Anthony Wood observed in 1678 that the local population was plagued by 'colds without coffing or running at the nose, onlie a languidness and faintness,' adding emphatically that 'certainly Oxford is no good aire'.

Low-lying, and infiltrated by running water, the place has found its climate vilified ever since. Cardinal Newman declared that 'the air of Oxford does not suit me. I feel it directly I return to it'; Thomas Hardy recoiled from 'an extinct air, accentuated by the rottenness of the stones'; while, in her 20th-century guide to the city, Jan Morris writes: 'For half the year it is a heavy, dank, enervating environment, and the damp seems to rot your energy, and surround you in a fog of permanent procrastination.'

Griffiths saw the value of his hotels plummet (the Angel from £22,500 to just £5,000 in 1850 and the Star from £15,500 to £6,000), and his distress was mirrored throughout the city. Young people emigrated for jobs, the working male population shrinking by around a thousand.

The railway gave town and gown another splendid opportunity for squabbling. The dons naturally threw up their port-stained hands at the suggestion of a station close to Magdalen Bridge, and that idea was neatly scuppered. They were similarly incensed when, in 1865, the GWR sought to transfer its carriage-making workshops to Oxford from Paddington (with the prospect of 1,500 jobs) and the Corporation offered the company a lease on Cripley Meadow, west of the centre.

The town was fervently in favour of the scheme, while gown opposition was led by Goldwin Smith, a history fellow at University College whose father had been a GWR director. In the event the company had a change of both management and mind, and the works moved to Swindon instead.

Dodgson in Wonderland

On a July day in 1862 the 30-year-old Christ Church maths tutor Charles Lutwidge Dodgson rowed up the Thames at Oxford with his friend Robinson Duckworth and the three young daughters of his college dean to enjoy a picnic on the bank upstream. On the way, he entertained the company with a richly imaginative story about a little girl and the strange world she discovers after falling down a rabbit hole.

Why not write it down? asked the 10-year-old Alice Liddell. And so it was that Dodgson, who had already published under his own name a highly regarded work on the ancient Greek mathematician Euclid, brought out *Alice's Adventures in Wonderland* and, later, *Through the Looking-Glass*, under the pseudonym Lewis Carroll.

Dodgson identified himself with the Dodo, the remains of which he would have seen in the new Oxford University Museum of Natural History (see page 172), and *Alice* aficionados find references to Oxford people and places throughout his works.

The books made him a lot of money, but he described their writing as 'a task where nothing of reward is hoped for but a little child's whispered thanks and the airy touch of a little child's pure lips'.

Carnage

By the end of the 19th century both the town and the university had recovered a good deal of their earlier prosperity and confidence, but disaster lay around the corner in the guise of 'the war to end all wars'.

In Field Marshal Haig (Brasenose), Oxford provided a leader historians have judged harshly for his handling of campaigns in which millions lost their lives. The city, along with its surrounding towns and villages, also provided its full complement of those victims. The Oxfordshire and Buckinghamshire Light Infantry, composed chiefly of local people, lost all of 15,878 members between 1914 and 1918.

The university, its undergraduates numbering no more than 3,000 year on year, lost almost 2,700 students, dons and college servants, and their names are inscribed on memorials in the individual colleges. At Christ Church the fatalities numbered 256, at New College 263 and at Keble 163. Brasenose lost more than a quarter of its 350 serving members. Sixteen Oxford men won the Victoria Cross.

Many of the young men who perished on a foreign field set off in a spirit of idealism. Julian Grenfell (Balliol), in his poem 'Into Battle', wrote 'Who dies fighting has increase.' The lines were published in *The Times* in May 1915 – together with the announcement of the poet's death.

The thrill of the Trill

T. E. Lawrence, later famous as 'Lawrence of Arabia' for his exploits during and after the First World War, displayed his adventurous spirit while a history undergraduate at Jesus by canoeing through the underground Trill Mill Stream – a rat-infested, brick-lined offshoot of the Thames once used as a sewer, which runs from the St Ebbe's area to emerge in Christ Church Meadow.

According to one friend (various accounts of the exploit surfaced later) he placed a candle in the bows of the canoe and an acetylene cycle-lamp at the stern, wondering which would gutter first in the foul air. He also carried a .45 revolver and a box of blanks, with the notion of firing through any gratings he came across in order to frighten the natives. 'Shooting the town drain' became popular with later students – until the authorities blocked off the entrances.

The age of petrol

In the aftermath of this terrible conflict an enterprising individual presented Oxford with something it had never known before – a genuine nuts-and-bolts, oil-and-grease, production-line industry.

The miracle worker was William Morris – not the Victorian artist, textile designer, writer and libertarian socialist (Exeter College), but the self-made former cycle mechanic (University of Life) who designed his first car, the Bullnose Morris, in 1912. After the war he picked up where he left off, and would eventually be turning out 1,000 vehicles a week from his Cowley works, on the site of a former military college to the southeast of the town.

Workers poured into the area in droves, with the GWR creating a new railway station to cope with the daily influx and private landlords falling over themselves to build homes for those wanting to settle. Wits with Paris in mind soon took to calling the university 'the left bank of Cowley'.

The factory made munitions in the First World War and de Havilland Tiger Moth training aeroplanes during the Second, but of course it's the cars for which the works became both famous and immensely profitable – among them the Morris Minor, the Morris Oxford and (best loved of all) the Mini.

Next door to Morris Motors was Pressed Steel, the car body manufacturing business set up by Morris and the American Budd Corporation in 1926 – and within ten years Oxford was home to the largest motor plant outside the USA.

The dour and practical Morris wasn't the kind of town representative the gowns were used to dealing with. He rather looked down his nose at academics, was prejudiced against university graduates on his staff and could be scathing about foreigners: 'Bonjour manure' was his idea of an amusing put-down. He had no children, and no interest but work. 'Those who disliked him speak ill of him,' wrote Jan Morris in her essential guide to Oxford, 'and those who were fond of him cannot find anything interesting to say.'

He was, however, fantastically generous with the immense fortune he amassed, his largesse being rewarded with a baronetcy (1st Viscount Nuffield) and two peerages. He gave generously to hospitals, beginning with the new orthopaedic unit at Headington, to which he turned up unannounced with a large cheque in his hand.

Oxford on toast

His impact wasn't as profound as William Morris's, but Frank Cooper produced such delicious marmalade that his name, and the city's, are still known for it worldwide.

He inherited his father's grocery business at 83–84 High Street, but the turning point came on the day in 1874 that his wife Sarah-Jane made 76 lb (34 kg) of marmalade to her own recipe. It was so phenomenally popular that Cooper eventually built a large and impressive four-storey factory in Park End Street, close to the twin stations and goods yards of the GWR and LNWR.

Brown & Polson bought the company in 1964 and transferred production elsewhere – but they knew better than to change the brand name.

Some 20th-century highlights

1912 William Morris designs his first car in Oxford.

1924 The Museum of the History of Science opens in the Old Ashmolean Museum, Broad Street.

1933 At the Oxford Union, the university's debating society, the motion 'that this House will in no circumstances fight for its King and Country' is passed by 275 votes to 153 – sending shock waves around the world.

1938 Oxford Airport opens at Kidlington, 7 miles (11 km) north of the city.

1954 Roger Bannister runs the first sub-4-minute mile at the university's Iffley Road track, which is later renamed after him.

1965 The Museum of Modern Art (actually an art gallery, and now called Modern Art Oxford) is established in Pembroke Street.

1990 Oxford Science Park, home to more than 60 companies, opens at Littlemore.

1992 Oxford Business Park is created on the former Morris Motors site at Cowley.

The aim of his Nuffield Foundation, established in 1943 with an endowment of £10 million, is today flagged as 'improving social well-being through education, research and innovation' (Morris was reportedly unhappy when it helped pay for the radio telescope at Jodrell Bank), while Nuffield College, founded in 1958, is a graduate college of the university which specialises in the social sciences.

On Morris's death in 1963 his home near Henley-on-Thames, Nuffield Place, passed to the college. It's now in the hands of the National Trust, which describes it as a time capsule of 1930s country-home living, displaying the relatively modest personal possessions, decor and furnishings of 'one of the richest men in the world' just as he and Lady Nuffield left them.

Morris Minor 1000

The company's fortunes rose and fell over the years, until only one of its brands remained in Oxford – and that in revamped guise:

- In 1952 Morris Motors merged with its great rival in the small car market, Austin, to form BMC – making Morris, MG, Riley and Wolseley vehicles.

- In 1968 it became part of British Leyland (BL), and some 20,000 people worked here and at the Pressed Steel Fisher site next door. The last Morris-badged passenger car was the Ital, made at Cowley until 1982 and then at Longbridge (Birmingham) until 1984.

- The plant closed in the early 1990s after prolonged difficulties in the British motor industry, although the site's transformation into the Oxford Business Park is something of which Morris would surely have approved.

- Meanwhile, cars continue to be made by BMW on the old Pressed Steel land. In August 2011 it produced its two-millionth new Mini on the site within ten years.

Morris had, for good or ill, achieved a remarkable transformation, turning a rather sleepy university city into an industrial centre with dons attached.

Academic exercise

Before the facility was closed down in 1991, generations of male academics would regularly strip to their bare nothings to take a dip in the Cherwell at the spot known as Parson's Pleasure in the southeast corner of the Parks – one of the few places in Britain where nude bathing was allowed.

Although it was possible for sensitive river users to skirt the area by getting out of their punts and hauling them over rollers behind a concealing fence, many an unsuspecting female pleasure-boater would blush to her roots as she glided past such extreme demonstrations of scholarly detail.

It's an Oxford legend that on one such occasion all the dons rushed to cover their genitals, except for the characterful classics professor Maurice Bowra, who instead draped a flannel over his head. When asked why, he's said to have replied: 'I don't know about you, gentlemen, but I'm best known in the town for my *face*.'

The Cutteslowe walls

Gated estates for the well-heeled have become commonplace in the modern era, but north Oxford had an early, and much reviled, example to the east of Banbury Road. Here, in 1934, the council built its Cutteslowe estate – and here, next door, Clive Saxton's Urban Housing Company put up private houses whose owners were thought to be in need of protection from the perceived 'slum dwellers' next door.

Massive brick walls with revolving iron spikes on the top were built across two of the new thoroughfares, the northern one splitting what became Wolsey and Carlton Roads, the southern blocking Aldrich from Wentworth. The no. 2 bus had two separate routes, one servicing each estate, and for those on the 'wrong' side of the divide there was a long walk around the 'right' side to reach the shops in Banbury Road.

This, for once, was no town vs. gown affair, but a snobbishness which separated the middle and working classes. In 1936, communist leader Abe Lazarus (popularly known as Bill Firestone after organising a strike at the Firestone Rubber Company in London) led a crowd of protesters to the walls, some wielding pickaxes – enraged locals, ward councillors, left-wing dons, idealistic undergraduates. The police dispersed them.

Two years later the council had the walls removed, but the High Court ruled that it had no right to do so, and the monstrosities were re-erected, spikes and all. It wasn't until 1959, after the council had compulsorily purchased them, that they were at last toppled for good.

Wot ~ no bombs?

Why didn't Hitler bomb Oxford? In the so-called 'Baedeker' raids of 1942 the Germans targeted tourist towns such as Bath, Exeter and York in retaliation for the Allies' destruction of Lübeck, but Oxford was left alone.

It's often said that the Führer spared the city because he planned to set up his capital here after his invasion of Britain – but, alas, no evidence has ever been found to support this beguiling claim.

Some Oxford curiosities

Dr Johnson's teapot
The writer and dictionary compiler came down from Pembroke without a degree because he ran out of money, but he left the college his teapot. Boswell said it held two quarts (2.3 litres).

Europe's last dodo
The stuffed bird came to the Ashmolean in 1659 from the collection of the naturalist John Tradescant the Younger, but only a dried skull and foot now survive in the University Museum of Natural History.

The Magdalen deer
As if the riverside walk and the magnificent bell tower weren't enough, the herd of fallow deer is an outrageous case of one-upmanship.

The Worcester lake
All that remains of the former Castle Mill Stream, it's the only lake to be found in the grounds of an Oxford college.

Percy Shelley's memorial
Hidden away in University College is a life-size marble figure of the drowned poet, designed for his grave in the Protestant Cemetery at Rome – which declined it. The snub was par for the course, because Shelley himself had been sent down from the college after denying authorship of an atheistic pamphlet.

The Alfred Jewel
This treasure of the Ashmolean Museum dates from the reign of Alfred the Great and is inscribed with the words AELFRED MEC HEHT GEWYRCAN – 'Alfred had me made'.

Brasenose knocker
The 'brazen nose' which gives the college its name is a knocker hanging above the high table in the dining hall. The story goes that it was taken off to Stamford, Lincolnshire, in the 14th century, that the girl's school to which it was affixed came up for sale in 1890 – and that the college bought the property solely to get their prized possession back.

The Headington shark
How weird to see a shark apparently embedded, head down, in a roof at no. 2 New High Street, Headington! It was designed by John Buckley in 1986 for local radio presenter Bill Heine. The council tried to have the popular sculpture removed, but it was eventually sanctioned at government level.

'The most English of all cities. Mother Oxford, Venus-Minerva, triple-haunted, hundred-tongued.'

John Fowles

A high old time

A visit to Oxford really ought to include one of its traditional festivities, so here's a short list for your diary:

May Morning at Magdalen

This is a special day in the city, with many pubs open from sunrise and some college bars (as you might expect) open all night. Thousands gather on Magdalen Bridge to hear madrigals sung from the roof of the college tower during the morning. There's morris dancing, too – starting in Radcliffe Square and then moving all over the place.

Beating the Bounds

Ascension Day (the fifth Thursday after Easter) is the time for confirming the ancient parish boundaries. After short services at St Michael at the North Gate and St Mary the Virgin, clergy and civic dignitaries parade around the landmarks, beating them with white wands, marking them with chalk and calling out 'Mark! Mark! Mark!' Both processions pass through Brasenose and end at Lincoln, where the participants are regaled with ivy beer.

Eights Week

This boisterous college event on the Isis in May runs from Wednesday to Saturday during the fifth week of Trinity term. There are separate divisions for men's and women's coxed eights, with something like 170 boats and about 1,500 rowers taking part.

In heats involving 13 crews at a time, the boats line up downstream and, on the firing of a cannon, each tries to 'bump' (overtake) the one in front while avoiding being caught by the one behind. The boats involved in a bumping drop out of the race and switch places the following day, while the crew behind can surge past to catch the next one in front and so 'overbump'. The aim is to become Head of the River, allowing the triumphant oarsmen and women to commission 'winning blades' in their college colours, inscribed with the names and weights of the crew.

St Giles Fair

Here's a shindig which closes St Giles and parts of Banbury Road and Woodstock Road for two whole days in early September – and has done for centuries.

At one time enterprising local householders hanging a bough of a tree over their front doors were allowed to sell beer and spirits to thirsty revellers, while anyone owning a beershop could bring barrels in to add to the general merriment. Occasional attempts to have the fair closed down for its riotousness thankfully came to nothing, and its noisy, colourful mishmash of gewgaw stalls and funfair rides is here to stay.

What's on

In 1964 the idealistic, shambling, generous and unpredictable John Rose (1925–2004) founded *Daily Information*, a brightly coloured, poster-sized sheet of event listings, advertisements, reviews and lively editorials.

This invaluable guide can still be consulted in colleges and local businesses, although it now appears only on Tuesdays, Thursdays and Saturdays in term time and on Fridays during vacations.

Rose set up Oxford's first drop-in computer centre and its first Internet cafe, so it's fitting that his creation is now also available online: www.dailyinfo.co.uk

The Boar's Head Feast

You'll have to inveigle yourself into Queen's College for this Christmas delight, based on the legend of a student who was attacked by a wild boar while reading Aristotle. He had the wit to thrust the book down the beast's throat, crying 'Graecum est!' – roughly translated as 'It's all Greek to me.'

At the feast in honour of this resourceful undergraduate, three chefs bring a boar's head into the hall, accompanied by torch bearers and a choir performing the 15th-century Boar's Head Carol. Members of the choir receive herbs from the platter, and the solo singer is rewarded with an orange from the boar's mouth.

With publishing, information technology and science-based industries alongside its motor manufacturing, Oxford has at least one foot firmly in the modern world – but it can never resist that longing look over its shoulder!

Glossary

(See also pages 78–79)

Anglo-Saxon Chronicle An anonymous history of England, begun in the 9th century and subsequently updated by various authors.

bastion A projecting part of a fortification.

beadle or **bedel** A college usher or security officer.

burgess A representative of a medieval town or borough.

burh A Saxon fortified town.

copyright library In the UK, one of six entitled to a free copy of every book published.

Corn Laws 19th-century legislation to restrict imports of grain and so protect the income of farmers.

Curia The governing body of the Roman Catholic Church.

Danegeld In Anglo-Saxon England, money paid as a bribe to Viking invaders.

Danelaw The area of northern England ruled by the Danes before the Norman Conquest.

Dissolution of the Monasteries The forced closure of monasteries and confiscation of their lands under Henry VIII in the 1530s.

fee farm In medieval times, land for which the tenant occupier paid an annual rent.

fellow A member of the governing body of the university or of one of its colleges.

guild A medieval union of craftsmen or traders.

indulgence A document issued by the medieval Church, certifying that a person has been excused penance for a misdemeanour.

interdict An order from the Church excluding a person or persons from the celebration of certain Christian rites, as a punishment for a serious misdemeanour.

livery A distinctive uniform worn by the servants of a particular family or institution.

motte-and-bailey A Norman castle consisting of two mounds within a ditch, the larger (the motte) surmounted by a wooden tower (the keep).

Oxonian A native, inhabitant or student of Oxford.

psalter A book of psalms.

quadrangle (usually abbreviated to **quad**) A central square, usually lawned, between ranges of buildings – a classic feature of Oxbridge colleges.

secular Not concerned with religion; *or* not living in an enclosed community such as a convent or monastery.

slighting Partial demolition of a building to make it unfit for use.

tonsured Having a partly shaved head, like a monk.

vill A medieval manor; an area of land roughly equivalent to a parish.

Vulgate The Latin version of the Bible used by the Roman Catholic church.

wattle and daub Woven sticks and mud plaster, used to make infill panels in a timber-framed building.

An Oxford timeline

AD 878 King Alfred defeats the Danes and soon afterwards builds a burh at Oxford.

911 First mention of Oxford in the historical records.

c. 1000 St Michael at the North Gate built; its original tower survives and is Oxford's oldest building.

1002 St Bride's Day massacre: St Frideswide's church destroyed by fire.

1009 Vikings sack Oxford.

1016 English nobles meet at Oxford to confirm their allegiance to King Canute (Cnut).

1066 Norman Conquest. Soon after, Oxford is reduced to 'waste'.

1071 Robert d'Oyly begins building a motte-and-bailey castle.

1120 St Frideswide's is refounded as an Augustinian priory.

1129 Osney (or Oseney) Abbey founded.

c. 1130 Henry I builds Beaumont Palace (little trace of it survives today).

1133 Godstow Nunnery founded to the northwest of Oxford (ruins survive).

1138 Geoffrey of Monmouth compiles his *History of the Kings of Britain*.

1142 Queen Matilda makes her escape from the castle, besieged by rival monarch Stephen.

1154 The 'Anarchy' ends at Oxford when Stephen agrees to the succession of Matilda's son, Henry II.

c. 1155 Oxford is granted its first royal charter.

1167 English students forced out of Paris arrive in Oxford – and the university is born.

1190 Emo of Friesland is the first known overseas student.

1209 First recorded town and gown riot.

1258 Henry III cedes powers to the nobles under the Provisions of Oxford.

1264 Oxford becomes the unofficial capital of England during the Barons' Revolt.

1266 The townsmen pay heavy fines to the king for supporting the defeated Simon de Montfort.

1268 Oxford sends its first MPs to Parliament.

1280 Rewley Abbey founded, near the present railway station.

1288 Beginning of Merton's Mob Quad, claimed to be the oldest in the university.

1314 Edward II gives Beaumont Palace to the Carmelites.

1315–1317 'Great famine' devastates the city.

1326 Queen Isabella and the rebellious Roger Mortimer enter Oxford.

1348 Arrival of the Black Death.

1355 St Scholastica's Day riot between students and townsmen.

1382 First edition of John Wycliffe's Bible in English.

1427 The Divinity School (now attached to the Bodleian Library) is the university's first building.

1487 Lambert Simnel, son of an Oxford joiner, claims the throne of England – and is defeated.

1508 and 1517 Outbreaks of 'sweating sickness'.

1524 Cardinal Wolsey suppresses St Frideswide's Priory in order to build Cardinal College on the site.

1545 Henry VIII renames Wolsey's college Christ Church and makes its chapel the cathedral of the new diocese of Oxford.

1555–1556 The three Oxford Protestant martyrs are burned to death in Broad Street.

1581 Edmund Campion, a former fellow of St John's, is hanged, drawn and quartered for his Catholic faith.

1589 Four Catholics executed in Oxford.

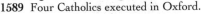

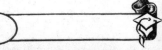

1602 Bodleian Library opens.

1610 Catholic missionary George Napier is hanged, drawn and quartered.

1621 Oxford University Botanic Garden opens.

1636 Oxford University Press is granted its charter by Charles I.

1642–1646 Charles I bases his court and army at Oxford during the Civil War.

1644–1646 Roundheads (Pariliamentarians) three times lay siege to the castle.

1645 Beheading of Archbishop Laud.

1652 Britain's first coffee shop opens in High Street.

1660 At the Restoration, Adrian Scrope (Hart Hall), a commissioner who signed Charles I's death warrant, is hanged, drawn and quartered.

1665–1666 Charles II brings his court to Oxford to escape the Plague in London.

1665 First edition of *The Oxford Gazette*, which later becomes *The London Gazette*.

1668 Christopher Wren's Sheldonian Theatre opens.

1677 Elias Ashmole gives the university his 'cabinet of curiosities', which becomes the nucleus of the Ashmolean Museum.

1681 Wren designs Tom Tower for Christ Church.

1683 Opening of the first Ashmolean Museum in Broad Street.

1715 Opening of Nicholas Hawksmoor's Clarendon Building for the Oxford University Press.

1729 The Wesley brothers and Oxford friends form the Holy Club – forerunner of the Methodists.

1748 Holywell Music Room opens.

1749 Radcliffe Camera built.

1774 Covered market opens north of High Street.

1790 Completion of the Oxford Canal.

1829 First Oxford vs. Cambridge boat race.

1832–1854 Three cholera outbreaks in the city.

1833 First of 90 tracts issued by the high church Oxford (or Tractarian) Movement.

1844 The railway comes to Oxford.

1845 Opening of the present Ashmolean Museum in Beaumont Street.

1854 The University Act removes religious tests for matriculation and bachelors' degrees.

1860 Great evolution debate in the new Museum of Natural History.

1871 Gladstone's Universities Tests Act removes religious tests from teaching posts.

1873 Work begins on new sewer system.

1875 New statute sanctions examinations for women.

1877 Universities of Oxford and Cambridge Act removes restriction of fellowships to clergymen – allowing dons to marry.

1878 Lady Margaret Hall becomes the first women's college at the university.

1879 Blackwell's bookshop opens.

1884 General Pitt Rivers donates his archaeological and anthropological collections to the university.

1886 Pitt Rivers Museum completed.

1893 New town hall built in St Aldate's.

1899 Ruskin College founded.

1902 First Rhodes Scholarships awarded.

1912 William Morris designs his first car in Oxford; he moves his business to Cowley in 1913.

1920 Women become full members of the university and are allowed to take degrees.

1924 Museum of the History of Science opens, in the Old Ashmolean building.

1933 'King and Country' debate at the Oxford Union.

1938 Oxford Airport opens at Kidlington.

1940 New Bodleian opens.

1942 Oxfam founded, as the Oxford Committee for Famine Relief.

1954 Roger Bannister runs sub-4-minute mile at the University Track (now Roger Bannister Track) in Iffley Road.

1959 Women's colleges awarded full collegiate status.

1965 Museum of Modern Art (now Modern Art Oxford) founded.

1974 First men's colleges accept women students.

1985 University refuses honorary degree to Prime Minister Margaret Thatcher.

1990 Oxford Science Park opens.

1992 Oxford Brookes University founded.

1992 Oxford Business Park created.

1996 Saïd Business School opens.

1999 Landscape by Paul Cézanne stolen from the Ashmolean.

2001 Production of BMW Mini begins at Cowley.

2007 Oxford prison reopens as a luxury hotel.

2008 St Hilda's, founded as a women's college in 1893, admits male students for the first time – the last college in the university to become mixed.

2009 Ashmolean Museum reopens after a major refurbishment.

2013 Ashmolean acquires John Everett Millais's portrait of John Ruskin.

2015 New Bodleian due to reopen as the Weston Library after extensive refurbishment.

2016 Students lead a campaign to have a statue of the controversial businessman, politician and British imperialist Cecil Rhodes removed from Oriel College, but as of 2017 the statue remains in place.

Index

The Cherished Library

Edited by Stephen Haynes and Nick Pierce

Available in hardback binding

Very Peculiar Histories™

at The Cherished Library

History of the British Isles
England (in 3 volumes)
   Vol. 1: From Ancient Times to Agincourt
     David Arscott   978-1-908973-37-5
   Vol. 2: From the Wars of the Roses to the
     Industrial Revolution *Ian Graham*   978-1-908973-38-2
   Vol. 3: From Trafalgar to the New Elizabethans
     John Malam   978-1-908973-39-9
   Boxed set of all three English volumes: 978-1-908973-41-2
Scotland (in 2 volumes) *Fiona Macdonald*
   Vol. 1: From Ancient Times to Robert the Bruce
      978-1-906370-91-6
   Vol. 2: From the Stewarts to Modern Scotland
      978-1-906714-79-6
   Boxed set of both Scottish volumes: 978-1-909645-03-5
Ireland *Jim Pipe*   978-1-905638-98-7
Wales *Rupert Matthews*   978-1-907184-19-2

History of the 20th century
Titanic *Jim Pipe*   978-1-907184-87-1
World War One *Jim Pipe*   978-1-908177-00-1
World War Two *Jim Pipe*   978-1-908177-97-1
The Blitz *David Arscott*   978-1-907184-18-5
Rations *David Arscott*   978-1-907184-25-3
Make-Do and Mend *Jacqueline Morley* 978-1-910184-45-5

Social history
Victorian Servants *Fiona Macdonald*   978-1-907184-49-9

North of the Border
Dundee *Fiona Macdonald*   978-1-910184-01-1
Edinburgh *Fiona Macdonald*   978-1-908973-82-5
Scottish Clans *Fiona Macdonald*   978-1-908759-90-0
Scottish Tartan and Highland Dress
 Fiona Macdonald   978-1-908759-89-4
Scottish Words *Fiona Macdonald*   978-1-908759-63-4
Whisky *Fiona Macdonald*   978-1-907184-76-5

Folklore and traditions
Christmas *Fiona Macdonald*   978-1-907184-50-5

British places
Brighton *David Arscott*   978-1-906714-89-5
Edinburgh *Fiona Macdonald*   978-1-908973-82-5
London *Jim Pipe*   978-1-907184-26-0
Oxford *David Arscott*   978-1-908973-81-8
The Thames *David Arscott*   978-1-912233-38-0
Yorkshire *John Malam*   978-1-907184-57-4

Famous Britons
Churchill *David Arscott*   978-1-912233-37-3
Great Britons *Ian Graham*   978-1-907184-59-8
Robert Burns *Fiona Macdonald* 978-1-908177-71-1
Charles Dickens *Fiona Macdonald* 978-1-908177-15-5
William Shakespeare *Jacqueline Morley* 978-1-908177-15-5

Sports and pastimes
Cricket *Jim Pipe*   978-1-908177-90-2
Gardening *Jacqueline Morley* 978-1-909645-19-6
Golf *David Arscott*   978-1-907184-75-8

Royalty
Kings & Queens of Great Britain
   Antony Mason   978-1-906714-77-2
Royal Weddings *Fiona Macdonald* 978-1-912233-96-0
The Tudors *Jim Pipe*   978-1-907184-58-1

Natural history
Cats *Fiona Macdonald*   978-1-908973-34-4
Dogs *Fiona Macdonald*   978-1-908973-35-1

Ancient and medieval history
Ancient Egypt: Mummy Myth and Magic
   Jim Pipe   978-1-906714-92-5
Castles *Jacqueline Morley*   978-1-907184-48-2

This is Volume 44 of A Very Peculiar History at The Cherished Library. A list of authors and their works in this series will be found on the preceding pages. The publishers will be pleased to send freely to all applicants an illustrated catalogue of the Library and our many other publications.

Book House
25 Marlborough Place
Brighton
BN1 1UB

www.salariya.com

Some reviews of other volumes in this series

Brighton by David Arscott
'a little gem' R. Cornaby
'light hearted but well researched' Wendy J

Whisky by Fiona Macdonald
'good-humoured, well researched . . . I stand in awe of the author's productivity.' Ian Buxton

10136 - OXFORD. HIGH STREET.